Novato New
808 Mulvey,
Mulvey, Dan
Write on!
31111027254034

P9-CEM-795

Write On!

Dan Mulvey, M.A.

Former English Teacher
Daniel Hand High School
Madison, Connecticut

BARRON'S

Acknowledgments

Page 157: "Fog" from *The Complete Poems of Carl Sandburg*, copyright 1970. Reprinted with permission by Harcourt, Inc.

Page 219: "The Hangman at Home" from *The Complete Poems of Carl Sandburg*, copyright 1970. Reprinted with permission by Harcourt, Inc.

© Copyright 2006 by Barron's Educational Series, Inc.

Illustrated by Tracy Hohn

All rights reserved. No part of this book may be reproduced in any form, by photostat, microfilm, xerography, or any other means, or incorporated into any information retrieval system, electronic or mechanical, without the written permission of the copyright owner.

All inquiries should be addressed to:
Barron's Educational Series, Inc.
250 Wireless Boulevard
Hauppauge, New York 11788
www.barronseduc.com

Library of Congress Control Number 2005058162

ISBN-13: 978-0-7641-3234-6
ISBN-10: 0-7641-3234-2

Library of Congress Cataloging-in-Publication Data
Mulvey, Dan.
      Write on! / by Dan Mulvey.
         p. cm.
      ISBN-13: 978-0-7641-3234-6
      ISBN-10: 0-7641-3234-2
       1. English language—Rhetoric. 2. English language—Grammar.
      3. Report writing. I. Title.

      PE1408.M747   2006
      808'.042—dc22   2005058162

Printed in the United States of America

9 8 7 6 5 4 3 2 1

Contents

PREFACE

Write On! is a handy reference for writing as well as a review of grammatical techniques for those needing direction in writing memos, directives, letters, essays, short stories, novels, biographies, autobiographies, and more. It is aimed at students in high school and college, as well as anyone else with an interest in improving writing skills. Middle school students who read well will also benefit. Not intended to be read from cover to cover— though you can, if you wish—this manual of writing is a handy reference for schools, businesses, and anyone interested in language and writing, whether versed in grammar or not.

It's generally best to get to the heart of the matter quickly. In writing, that's knowing when to use active and passive voices. So that's where this book begins. What is it that gives your writing punch? Then we backtrack a bit to review grammar basics and define terms. Syntax follows. Knowing the best way to arrange a sentence can make a good writer great and a great writer legendary. From sentences we proceed to paragraphs and beyond. And, of course, we can't forget punctuation.

Throughout this guide, you will find information on

- major errors in composition and speech, and common usage errors to avoid
- selection of topics on which to write
- use of figurative language, language that elevates one's writing
- different levels of language
- great authors whose writing is varied enough to help in developing your own style

The last chapter in this book is a test of common writing mistakes. If you score less than 80 percent, keep this book handy!

Write On! contains an extensive appendix. There is an "improve your vocabulary" program that will help you write, speak, listen, and read better. You'll find lists of pronouns, transitional expressions, parts of irregular verbs, conjugations of irregular verbs, prepositions, stories about words and incidents experienced by the author, a glossary of grammatical terms for quick reference, comparative and superlative forms of adjectives, a reading program, and answers to a *who, whom* quiz.

Write On! is your stepping stone to better writing. Write On!

ACKNOWLEDGMENTS

I have to thank, first and foremost, my wife, Nancy, for putting up with my "writing phases" that get me up at all hours of the nights and early mornings. Gerry Degenhardt, my former colleague and longtime friend, who not only edited but encouraged and contributed to *Write On!* I could not write without. I cannot forget my former students who contributed: Bonnie Leigh; her sister Roxie; Matt Decapua; Amy and Emily Jirsa; Kaili Floyd, the youngest contributor; Lisen Connery; Dr. Tom Suchanek, an author in his own right; and Stephanie Gay, who flies Navy jets. I also thank Ray Dudley, for letting me use his classroom, and his student Becky Jablonski, who will be a senior at Daniel Hand High School when this book arrives.

Linda Turner, my editor both on *Write On!* and *Grammar the Easy Way*, must have patience enough for a city of authors and knows how to redirect my often misdirected thinking. Of course, Wayne Barr, the acquisitions manager at Barron's, who gives me chances to write and shares with me the wisdom of Mark Twain; Veronica Douglas who is always friendly and encouraging.

And to all my friends who encourage and remind (not to forget their names in the text).

A Word that breathes distinctly
Has not the Power to die

Emily Dickinson

Chapter One

KNOWING THE DIFFERENCE BETWEEN ACTIVE AND PASSIVE VOICE

Active: The car crashes into the building.

Passive: The stalled car was kicked by the owner.

An essay by Laura Vanderkam in *USA Today* began with an anecdote about Ariel Horn, an English teacher/writer, who in her junior year of high school received a B+. Dismayed, indignant, and angry that the teacher did not recognize her genius, Ms. Horn found out her literary genius was clouded by grammatical errors—particularly because her essay featured more passive than active verbs. She rewrote the essay, corrected her errors, and even today claims that she cannot use the passive voice—ever.

Why then do students depend on the passive voice? If, when developing a paragraph, they would think about making a movie and the director who shouts "Action!" they might think "Action!" and use the active voice. Passive voice can be used in certain circumstances, but the active voice is what makes writing, and reading, interesting.

Any passive voice or a "be" verb can be turned into the active voice. Also, using the active voice gives the writer thousands more choices since there are a limited number of "be" verbs. Look at the examples that follow:

> **Passive:** Beth Etzel *had been told* that her son Simon was the best English student.
>
> **Active:** Mr. Gerald Degenhardt *told* Beth Etzel that her son Simon was the best English student.
>
> **Passive:** The house *was built* by Bruce Lockhart.
>
> **Active:** Bruce Lockhart *built* his own house.
>
> **Passive:** Roberta Lockhart *was raised* in Columbus, Ohio.
>
> **Active:** Jim and Eleanore Timko *raised* their daughter Roberta in Struthers, Ohio.

Passive: The best eggplant dish in the world *is made* by Helen Lockhart.

Active: Helen Lockhart *prepares* the best eggplant dish in the world.

Is there a case for the passive voice and "be" verbs as the main verbs? Absolutely, and after a discussion of the active voice (see Appendix Four for the conjugation of all the moods and voices), I will try to show when the passive or the "be" verbs can be sprinkled into one's writing. Just so there is no confusion, I present further examples:

Active: Molly *lambasted* Chris because he wrote nasty things on her wagon.

Passive: Chris *was lambasted* by Molly because he wrote nasty things on her wagon.

Active: Chris Simmons *graduated* Cum Laude from a major university.

Passive: Chris Simmons *was awarded* the Scholar's Book for her achievements in college.

Active: Young Mike Simmons *wrestled* an alligator on a farm in Florida.

Passive: Young Mike Simmons *was defeated* by an alligator on a farm in Florida.

Active: On Middle Beach Road, old Mike Simmons *constructed* a house that was nicknamed the Taj.

Passive: Old Mike Simmons *is known* for his riotous outbreaks during church services.

Active: Ginny Simmons *galavants* all over the world.

Passive: Ginny Simmons *was talked* into a trip to Ukraine.

Get the idea? In the active voice sentences, the subject is performing the action, while in the passive sentences, the subject has something happening to him or her. The action verbs move forward rather than backward. Passive verbs slow things up because events signified by the verbs revert to the subject rather than progress to the next step.

"Be" (*is, am, are, was, were,* and *been*) verbs really are not needed as main verbs but are needed with present and past participles to form the progressive mood and the passive voice.

As the main verb: Former President Clinton *is* now a famous author.

Notice how *is,* a "be" verb, is not needed in the following sentence:

Former President Clinton, now a famous author, interviewed well on *60 Minutes.*

As helping verbs for the progressive mood:

Tom Rylander *is* currently thinking about running for President in the near future.

or

Lenny Wilkens *was* considering retirement until the Knicks offered him the job of head coach.

or

Paige Cahill *will be* applying to North Carolina State, where her grandfather, Ed Bartels, starred in basketball.

Note: The progressive mood uses the present participle (the –*ing* form of the verb) and indicates an action that continues over an indefinite period of time.

Question: Is the active voice more powerful than "be" verbs as the main verbs in sentences?

The following paragraphs might not only answer the question but also show the benefits for using the active voice. The first contains almost all "be" verbs:

> The gray heron is on the bank of the Hammonassett River. A mother mallard and two youngsters are in the middle of the river checking out bread look-alikes. An ibis is on the far bank looking for fiddler crabs that are near their holes. A cormorant is up for air with an eel that did not get away. Over to the left on the man-made platform, an osprey mother is with her two newborns, while father osprey is on the nearby pole watching. An oystercatcher is on the edge of the low-water mark. A large egret is walking in a stately manner. A nuthatch on a nearby red oak is watching river morning.

Comment: The scene is nice, but it needs something more. Notice what happens when action verbs take the place of the "be" verbs:

> Looking for breakfast, the long-time resident gray heron struts along the bank of the Hammonassett River. A mother mallard and two of her surviving youngsters glide along checking out bread scrap look-alikes. An ibis balances on one leg, seemingly asleep, but ready for a tasty fiddler crab that has wandered too far from its hole. A cormorant surfaces silently with a wriggling eel that will not be wriggling long. Over to the left

on the man-made platform, a mother osprey feeds two young-sters a delicious flounder just snagged, while father osprey looks on proudly. An oystercatcher scurries along the low-water mark, pecking here and there for snails, just as a large egret, carefully choosing his own steps, prepares to spear an errant snapper that has roamed too far from school. A nuthatch, which looks as if he is perched the wrong way on the far red oak, watches river morning.

Answer: The liveliness of language comes from the action verbs.

THE CASE FOR PASSIVE VOICE

Since the passive voice does exist, the reason for its existence must rate some discussion. Certainly, scientific reports use the passive voice because usually the subject acted upon outweighs the importance of who does the research or who finds things out. Read in some magazines, if you can without glasses or even a magnifying glass, the technical information about Allegra (The passive voice and the "be" main verbs are underlined):

Reports of fexofenadine hydrochloride overdose <u>have been</u> infrequent. . . . However, dizziness, drowsiness, and dry mouth <u>have been reported</u>. Single doses of FH . . . <u>were administered</u>. . . .

and

Dose-related decreases in pup weight gain and survival <u>were observed</u> in rats. . . .

and

The recommended dose in patients 6 to 11 years <u>is based</u> on cross-study comparison. . . .

Not the most interesting reading. Perhaps the persons who write this information know that no one will read the text anyway.

Another use of the passive voice might occur if the "agent" of the sentence is an indefinite pronoun (*someone*, *nobody*, *anyone*) or *people*:

Nobody has been named to take the vacancy left by the Superintendent of Schools after he was accused of embezzlement.

People have been noticed loitering near the Island Avenue School.

What stands out as one major use of the passive smacks of deceit politically. This trickery might sound something like

The President *was advised* that there were definite signs of weapons of mass destruction hidden in Iraq.

Notice how, if indeed there were (or not) weapons found (or not), the President shoulders no fault, but the advisor is nowhere to be found.

Two experts, H. W. Fowler (and R. W. Burchfield) and William Strunk Jr. (and E. B. White) in *Fowler's Modern English Usage* and *Elements of Style* agree that although "the active voice is usually more direct and vigorous than the passive," this rule does not mean that the writer eschew the use of the passive voice, which is often useful and necessary.

Therefore, use the active voice for essays, novels, plays, biographies, and autobiographies (especially you high school students who have the difficult task of impressing an admissions director with your autobiography or an essay depicting who influenced you the most) and limit the use of the passive. Use the passive when it is imperative to draw attention to the agent acted upon rather than the subject, when the actor in the sentence is unimportant, if the agent is indefinite, or when you wish to put the blame on someone else.

Be precise with language: Use the active voice, and get those six figures, or go to Providence College, or even Yale—then get a six figure salary and retire early.

Publication—is the Auction
Of the Mind of Man—
                              Emily Dickinson

Chapter Two

LITTLE AND BIG PARTS OF WRITING

"There's a Claus on the roof!"
"Adjective or adverb?"

WORDS, PHRASES, CLAUSES

Most writers as students begin their journey with a study of THE PARTS OF SPEECH and immediately raise one eyebrow and think to themselves, "What does *speech* have to do with writing? Why not call these things THE PARTS OF WRITING and move on?" Also, these "parts" are sometimes assumed to be one word like *wedding* (noun), *large* (adjective), *succinctly* (adverb), and so on.

However, most grammarians and English teachers know that nouns, pronouns, verbs, adjectives, adverbs, prepositions, conjunctions, and interjections—these beginnings of the teaching and learning of grammar, THE BIG EIGHT—are not limited to being just a word. In the following examples, all the underlined parts function as **nouns**, defined as the names of persons, places, things, qualities, or ideas:

A. Ron Freytag's biggest <u>pleasure</u> centered around his <u>experiences</u> in the <u>Bronx</u>. (And if Ron Freytag did not have an apostrophe connected with his name, he would be underlined also.)

B. <u>To ski Chamonix</u> (subject) with <u>Gregory Mulvey</u> (object of the preposition) remained my biggest <u>thrill</u> (predicate noun).

C. By <u>grimacing for almost a minute</u> (noun phrase), <u>Matthew</u> (subject), <u>one of the world's great soccer players</u> (appositive phrase), led his <u>coach</u> (direct object) to believe there was something wrong.

D. <u>Whoever took Jonathan's new driver</u> (noun clause) had better put it back.

Once the premise that six of the parts of speech can be a single word *or* a group of words (pronouns except for *no one* and correlative conjunctions *either . . . or* and *not only . . . but also*), the student and the teacher of English grammar, which seems to be taught less today than before, break through an ancient barrier and learn once and for all this stuff of words. Grammar is easy*, but, in fact, many students learn their grammar by taking French, Spanish, German, or some other foreign language—not in their English class. To continue . . .

The following underlined parts are **adjectives** (words, phrases, or clauses that modify, change, limit, or describe a noun or pronoun), again not limited to just one word:

> A. George W. Bush, <u>who, many believe, lied to Americans about weapons of mass destruction in Iraq</u>, continued to spout <u>his</u> <u>own</u> <u>justifiable</u> rhetoric. ("His" doubles as a possessive, which is both adjective and pronoun. Without this word, the writer would of necessity keep repeating GWB's name.)
>
> B. <u>Writhing after reading Louis Menard's scathing review in *The New Yorker*,</u>

Lynne Truss finally took <u>a</u> <u>deep</u> breath and chuckled all the way to <u>the</u> banque.

Adverbs (words, phrases, or clauses that modify, change, describe, or limit verbs, adjectives, or other adverbs) we were taught ended mostly in *-ly*, but now we know, based on the information above, that adverbs come in all different shapes and sizes, and many times with no *-ly*:

*See *Grammar the Easy Way* by this author (Barron's, 2002).

A. <u>When Katie Couric interviewed Michael Moore about his new film _Fahrenheit 9/11_</u> (adverb clause), <u>in a non sequitur</u> (adverb phrase) she mentioned that he did <u>not</u> (one word adverb) seem to spend much money <u>on his wardrobe</u> (adverb phrase).

Note: As the first lesson in grammar ran into the second week or so, we as students studied prepositions. (See Appendix Five for a complete list of prepositions.) Some teachers even made us memorize the lot of them, but when we arrived at the "phrase stage" of our lesson, we found out that prepositions never exist by themselves. They "joined" a noun or pronoun with some other word in a sentence (<u>went</u> _to_ the <u>movies</u>, the <u>boy</u> _in_ the <u>bubble</u>). In fact, prepositions need a noun or a pronoun and sometimes an adjective or adverb or two to give them life. Moreover, then we found out that prepositional PHRASES are either adjectives or adverbs. No wonder many students do not get the concept the first time around!

B. I went to college <u>to learn journalism</u>, but I <u>really</u> wanted to play professional baseball. (Recognizable as an adverb, of course, is "really" because it ends in "-_ly_." The infinitive phrase "to learn journalism" modifies the verb "went" and is also an adverb.)

Note: One-word adjectives function three ways: to describe a noun (_the crusty old_ sportswriter), to describe a noun comparatively (the _more handsome, cuter,_ and _more sophisticated_ teacher of the two responsible for World Studies 1), and to describe the ultimate of a group (the _most derelict, vilest, most offensive_ bartender of any in town). See Appendix Eight for further explanation.

When we as students learned that a **verb** is an action word, we might have been thrown off, too. Then when we learned our conjugations (see the Appendix Four for a complete scheme of conjugations) and arrived at the future perfect (*will have been elected, shall have been shelved*), suddenly the one-word verb changed majestically into four words. What is going on here! Then we remembered the premise: With perhaps the exception of the coordinating conjunction (*and, but, or nor, for, yet*), all parts of WRITING, including the correlative conjunctions (*either . . . or, neither . . . nor, not only . . . but also, whether . . . or, both . . . and*) can be more than just one word.

Even **prepositions** (words that link a noun or pronoun with some other word) like

<u>according to</u>, <u>because of</u>, <u>by way of</u>, <u>in regard to</u>, and <u>out of</u>

are made up of more than just one word.

The **interjection** (a part of speech that indicates emotion or interruption) also can comprise a few words as in the following examples:

A. Oh my God!

B. Gee whiz!

C. Shiver me timbers!

It seems that the study of grammar might begin with something other than "This is a noun."

PHRASES

By grammatical definition, a **phrase** is a group of words functioning as a part of speech (usually a noun, an adjective, or an adverb), without a subject or a verb. Incidentally, recognizing these larger-than-one-word parts of speech tends to increase students' reading ability as well as improve their writing because they begin to see the larger units with only one eye movement.

Let's start with the **prepositional phrase**. Certainly if you analyzed a piece of writing, you would find prepositional phrases abundant. A prepositional phrase has two or three parts: It always ends with a noun or pronoun (NEVER END A SENTENCE WITH A PREPOSITION echoes in every English classroom), and it functions as an adjective or an adverb. Long prepositional phrases at the beginning of a sentence usually are set off by commas, and prepositional phrases that begin a sentence are almost always adverbs. Notice the following examples:

A. *Into the Wild, Into Thin Air,* and *Under the Banner of Heaven* (three books written by Jon Krakauer)

Only the last example has a prepositional phrase used as an adjective—"of Heaven" describes "Banner" (a noun), but the other prepositional phrases are neither adjective nor adverb because they do not attach themselves to any other words. In sentences, prepositional phrases that are not titles of books (example B) are attached to some other word in the sentence (examples C, D, and E). Prepositional phrases are adjectives or adverbs, depending on their use.

B. *Moyers on America*—"on America" describes "Moyers," a noun, and therefore is an adjective.

C. *In Herman Melville's novel about the hunting of whales,* the author also <u>gives</u> the reader a short lesson *on cetology,* the science *of whales.* (Notice that the long series of prepositional phrases modify "gives" and are set off by a comma.)

D. the <u>boy</u> *in the red flannel shirt* ("in the red flannel shirt" describes "boy" and therefore is an adjective because "boy" is a noun.)

E. <u>Teaching</u> *in American high schools* today demands extraordinary <u>energy</u> *from educators*. (Both phrases are adjectives modifying "Teaching" and "energy," both nouns.)

These next phrases, the participial, gerund, and infinitive phrases, in ancient times (and sometimes today) were called verbals. Like the shampoo Herbal Essence, which never had a real herb even close to it, verbals are not verbs at all, but they do look like verbs just as Herbal Essence smells like herbs.

The **participial phrase** transforms verb forms into adjectives. Past participles end in *-d*, *-ed* (as in most regular verbs like *looked*, *braked*), *-n* (*thrown*), *-en* (*shaven*), and *-t* (*went*, *brought*); some end in *-g* (*hung*, *slung*, *rung*); a couple, in *-k* (*drunk*, *struck*); and even some, in *-e* (*borne*, *gone*, *made*); and one ends in *-m* (*swum*). Present participles always end in *-ing*.

The past participle and the present participle can both be used as adjectives, and we will see the present participle used as a noun, as demonstrated later in this chapter.

A. <u>Spending money wisely</u>, Shauna Mulvey Fitzgerald passed on a deal that would have filled her house with twenty-five 100-amp speakers. (participial phrase modifying "Shauna")

B. Charles Dickens, <u>writing *Great Expectations*</u>, creates Pip as a naïve but lovable character. (participial phrase modifying "Dickens")

C. As Joan Venditto lauded her student with accolades seldom heard, the student, <u>struck dumb with wonder</u>, nearly fainted. (participial phrase modifying "student")

The present participle, used in the examples above, can be transformed into nouns (called gerunds). These **gerunds** can also be used in **phrases**.

A. <u>Spending money wisely</u> does not interest Shauna Mulvey Fitzgerald. (The same phrase that is an adjective above is now a noun—the subject of the sentence.)

B. By <u>writing *Great Expectations* with two endings</u>, Charles Dickens satisfied all of his readers. (the same phrase as the one above, but this phrase serves as a noun, the object of the preposition "by")

Infinitive phrases can serve as nouns, adjectives, or adverbs, but writers usually can use these parts of speech without knowing precisely what they are. Since they can usually be placed anywhere in the sentence, their use becomes easy. **Infinitives** are formed by attaching *to* with the present tense, and can be used by themselves—the most famous from Shakespeare: "To be or not to be"—or in phrases. The infinitive phrases in these examples are underlined:

A. <u>To awaken early on a spring day</u>, Peter Weiss set his alarm clock for 5:00 A.M.

B. Peter Weiss, <u>to awaken early on a spring day</u>, set his alarm clock for 5:00 A.M.

C. Peter Weiss set his alarm clock for 5:00 A.M. <u>to awaken early on a spring day</u>.

Appositives and appositive phrases help the writers at times by enabling them to toss in another bit of information without seeming repetitive; it is a noun renaming the noun it follows.

One-word appositive: My sister <u>Maureen</u> sometimes lives in Florida.

Appositive phrases: Larry Howard Lewis, <u>a die-hard Yankee fan</u>, wrinkles his nose at the name Red Sox.

CLAUSES

A **clause**, by definition, is a group of words containing a subject and a verb and functions as noun, adjective, or adverb. This unit, sometimes referred to as a dependent clause (as opposed to independent clauses, or sentences) cannot stand by itself but must be attached to some other word in the context.

Those dependent clauses written as sentences are called **fragments** (a group of words that looks like a sentence because of a capital letter and a period but usually is missing a verb or begins with a subordinating conjunction) and in formal prose should be avoided. Fiction writers use fragments (along with phrases and even words) all the time; however, it is not that they do not know the difference between a sentence and a fragment. We might even call it "writer's license." Some examples of fragments follow:

A. Because he rested on his laurels.
B. In the morning just after the sun came over the yardarm.
C. Whenever Helen Wilson throws a party at her house.

Noun clauses function five different ways, just as any noun does:

> **Subject:** <u>Whoever joins the union before the deadline of January 10</u> will reap many benefits.
>
> **Direct object:** Richie Hahn cut down <u>whichever tree shaded his immense garden</u>.
>
> **Indirect object:** Ray Dudley gave <u>whoever turned in a paper early</u> an extra credit.
>
> **Object of the preposition:** By <u>whatever was at hand</u>, Caitlin Crosbie Doonan constructed a sculpture that was bought by the Smithsonian.
>
> **Predicate noun:** Ahab's overwhelming manic idea was <u>that he destroy a white whale</u> (that was responsible for his missing leg). The second part of the predicate nominative is an adjective clause that becomes an integral part of the noun clause.

Noun clauses begin with the following words: *that, what, where, when, who, whom, which, whose, how, why, whether, whoever, whenever, whatever.*

Adjective clauses function as handy details. They almost always begin with certain words (*who, whom, which, that, whose*), they always come immediately after the noun or pronoun they modify, and sometimes they add a certain elegance to the style of the writer. Most adjective clauses can be reduced to phrases or even words, but sometimes an adjective clause is just what the language doctor ordered. Also, these clauses can be restrictive (essential) or nonrestrictive (nonessential) depending on the thought of the author.

The man <u>who loves words</u> is the man <u>who loves to read</u>. (Notice these two adjective clauses are not set off by commas because they are essential (restrictive) to the sentence—they cannot be left out without confusion because if they were left out the sentence would read "The man is the man," which might be heard on the street, but never written.)

Eric Jan Alen Axberg, <u>who owns a house in Madison, Connecticut</u>, is an expert at making glogg, a Norwegian Christmas drink. (Notice the commas around the clause; then read the sentence without the clause. The sentence still makes sense.) The clause is nonessential (nonrestrictive). It adds informational but not necessary information.

The use of *that* or *which* needs mentioning. *Which* will introduce a clause that is nonessential to the sentence:

> Shelly Marie Rochelle Axberg lives in a beautiful house, <u>*which* was a recent acquisition</u>, and she takes great pride in showing it off to even waitresses and bartenders.

That, on the other hand, usually introduces a clause that is essential to the sentence. Removing the clause would greatly alter the meaning intended:

> Wally Camp drives a car <u>*that* was given to him by his grandfather</u>.
>
> William Peter Brainerd is in the market for a camera <u>*that* takes better pictures</u> than the one he has now.

Note: Sometimes in an adjective clause the introductory word is left out. This occurs in the following two sentences:

James George McGuire is the person <u>I met</u> in the Blackstone Library. (The word *whom* is omitted probably because the author had no clue whether to use *who* or *whom*.)

In his living room, Don Johnson Floyd drives the tractor <u>he bought</u> at Sears. (The word "that" is omitted but could easily be inserted.)

One other note: Use *which* and *that* to refer to animals and inanimate objects and *who* or *whom* to refer to people. Mark Twain once said that the person who uses "that" to refer to a person is suspect.

Adverb clauses always begin with an adverbial conjunction that indicates the following:

Cause: <u>Because</u> Kevin Michael Blair has won many tennis tournaments, he has become a legend—in his own mind.

Concession: <u>Although</u> Charlie Rogers sports a white full beard, no one has asked him to play Santa Claus.

Condition: <u>If</u> Wanda Hughes married Henry Kissinger, she would be Wanda Hughes Kissinger now.

Place: <u>Wherever</u> Roger Marcio DeSousa goes, he goes by car.

Purpose: Bruce Schmottlach runs marathons <u>so that</u> his youthful appearance will stay with him.

Possibly the best thing about writing an adverb clause is that it rarely can be misplaced no matter where authors use it. Also, predictably, these clauses always begin with the following words: *after, although, as, as though, because, before, even though, if, in order that, since, so that, unless, until, where, wherever, when,* or *whether,* and perhaps a few others.

Well, now that you have mastered the basics of grammar, proceed to the next chapter and learn how to arrange these bits and pieces into some organized, well-thought-out, terrific sentences. See you in syntax.

Language is poetry when it makes my whole body so cold
No fire can ever warm me.

Emily Dickinson

Chapter Three

SENTENCES AND ARRANGEMENT OF BIG AND LITTLE PARTS OF SPEECH (IN OTHER WORDS, SYNTAX)

"Could have used some parallel structure here."

Have you ever tried to define syntax? There must be thousands of definitions, almost as many as there are English teachers. Stated simply, **syntax** is the arrangement of words so that one may communicate precisely through writing and/or speaking. Without certain rules, we would be faced with severe problems:

> Is of a sentence of to words relationships the syntax show within arrangement meaning.

This group of words would take too long to decipher; however, the meaning is fairly clear: Without syntax, we would all go around with blank stares. Let us rearrange the "sentence":

> Syntax is the arrangement of words to show relationships of meaning within a sentence.

If, then, arrangement is critical, let us put forth a series of arrangements for sentences so that when we write or say something, be it lengthy or terse, written or spoken, it is immediately understood (and remembered).

There are several categories of arrangement: parallel structure, correct arrangement of pronouns, agreement of the subject and verb, agreement of the pronoun and antecedent, correct placement of modifiers, placement of parts of speech, arrangements to vary sentences, and coordination–subordination.

PARALLEL STRUCTURE OR KEEPING LIKE SENTENCE ELEMENTS TOGETHER

Of all the arrangements that clear up thoughts and thinking, parallel structure ranks as the number one organizer. Simply put, parallel structure organizes details in sentences by arranging like sentence elements: In other words, noun phrases go with noun phrases, adjective clauses with adjective clauses, adverbs with adverbs, and so on. This technique is used primarily when the writer wishes to list two or more items—but at least two. Notice the blanks in the following sentences and mentally choose a word or group of words to complete the thought:

A. Bob Sembler, a physical therapist, stresses everyday workouts, encourages patients with positive reinforcement, and _____ .

B. By regaling customers with funny stories, by mixing drinks second to none, and _____ , Joe Gallagher epitomizes the great bartender.

C. Wally Camp, basketball coach extraordinaire, taught his players scare tactics, referee bating, jersey pulling, and _____ .

D. Rob Gourley, when he taught business administration at Durham High School, proposed that the curriculum be revised, that the school grounds be studied, and _____ .

In the A example, if you placed a verb first to go with "stresses" and "encourages," give yourself a pat on the back. Might this suggestion work: "works individually with each patient"?

In the B example, if you used the word "by" or at least another preposition to start with, you're right on the money. Might the following work: "by paying attention to details"?

In the C example, it's obvious that the blank should contain some kind of adjective–noun combination. If you said something like "crowd jeering," you did well.

In the D example, the obvious choice for the first word would be "that." If you said something like "that teachers be free to choose extracurricular activities," then you are becoming an expert in parallel structure.

So then, anytime two or more grammatical items are joined, we know they should be the same part of speech (remembering, of course, that parts of speech are made up sometimes with more than just a word). Look how the **correlative conjunctions** give syntax a boost by forcing the writer to use certain grammatical forms when joining just two items:

> **Neither . . . nor** Danny Fitzgerald neither <u>flinched</u> nor <u>ran</u> when faced with a huge brown bear.

> **Either . . . or** Either <u>we fight</u> or <u>we lose</u>. (Notice that after both parts of the correlative the same grammatical structure is used.)
>
> **Both . . . and** Caroline Fitzgerald both <u>walked</u> in the Mother's March against Cancer and <u>donated</u> her weekly allowances to the fund.

Not only . . . but also Josh Stone not only <u>drove</u> in the winning run with a triple but also <u>made</u> a shoestring catch to save the victory.

Whether . . . or Whether <u>John Rowland quit because he was guilty</u> or <u>he just did not want to face embarrassment</u> is for the voters to decide.

The same kind of arrangement writers can achieve by using **coordinating conjunctions.** These connecting words (*and, but, or, nor, for, yet*) can join two or more items, as many as the writer deems necessary. The following examples show how some of these conjunctions can join two, and then many, like grammatical items:

and (two items): Collin Sembler starred on his school's soccer team <u>and</u> showed superior defensive skills during the season.

and (a few items): Having two knees replaced, losing twenty-five pounds, changing completely his life style, <u>and</u> trading in his Model T for a brand-new Mustang, Dan basked in the compliments his friends bestowed.

but (two items): Carefully pronouncing his words <u>but</u> not concentrating on his thoughts caused Tom Purcell the loss of his audience.

but (many items): Legend has it that Babe Ruth ate twenty hot dogs once before a game, on several occasions loaded his bat with cork for more distance, stayed up all hours of the night during most days of the week, <u>but</u> never failed to delight the fans at Yankee Stadium.

or (two items): Proper etiquette <u>or</u> proper dress most employers demand during interviews.

or (many items): My aunt thought that raising a family, landing a huge job, finding the proper neighborhood, or joining a civic organization would be enough for success in a small town.

nor (almost always used with **neither**—but never **either**) See correlative conjunctions above.

for an interesting conjunction (and a preposition) used only as a joiner of two complete thoughts: Ralph Garcia studied classical Spanish, for he believed that that subject held life's truths.

yet (two items): Joel Davis, once principal of Durham High School, told his teachers that they should always be firm yet fair.

yet (many items): Bombastic, loud, obnoxious, yet always controlled, Chipper Williams loves being the chairman of the Dawn Patrol.

Parallel structure, then, is one way to achieve perfect syntax. By grouping like sentence elements, the writer conveys thoughts clearly so that the reader does not have to guess at meanings.

For those taking the SAT Writing Test: Recognition might not take the form of "Aha! That's parallel structure." To do well on writing skills questions, all one need remember are the signals: items in a series, correlative and coordinating conjunctions— search no further because those signals indicate the joining of like sentence elements.

CORRECT ARRANGEMENT (AND USE) OF PRONOUNS, OR MAKING SURE THE READER KNOWS TO WHAT OR WHOM THE PRONOUN REFERS

Discussion here focuses on ambiguous reference, weak reference, and indefinite reference. For general reference of pronouns, see Chapter Seven, Number One Usage Mistake to Avoid.

Ambiguous reference occurs when the use of the pronoun is unclear. In other words, the reader does not understand to which word to attach the pronoun.

A. Mary told her mother she should study more.

B. The first selectman said to the town engineer that he was doing a great job.

C. Loretta Kiku Blair once responded to a television reporter that he was great at what he did.

In every case, the reader has no idea about what the pronoun refers. Correcting these is easy: Get rid of the pronouns, or make the reference absolutely clear.

A. Mary said, "Mom, you should study more."

B. The first selectman lauded the town engineer on the latest project.

C. Loretta Kiku Blair praised the television reporter for the questions asked.

Weak reference occurs when there is no antecedent, no word to which the pronoun refers.

A. We searched in all the ponds at the golf course but could not find any. ("Golf balls" has to be there somewhere.)

B. Up and down the street we approached scalpers but none had one to give up (obvious: "ticket").

C. The usher helped us but there were none to be had ("seats," certainly not "peanuts").

Indefinite reference happens when the pronoun used seems to refer to an indefinite person or group. Usually the words *they* or *it* are involved.

    A. They say that "time assuages." (With an apology to Emily Dickinson, *who* say?)

    B. It said in the paper recently that smoking is detrimental to one's health. ("It"?)

    C. They say eating a low carb diet does more harm than good. (Doctors? Lawyers? English teachers?)

AGREEMENT OF SUBJECT AND VERB

This part of syntax, the agreement of subject and verb, gives beginning writers fits, probably because there are many restrictions. Basically, a verb must agree with its subject or subjects in number (singular or plural). Sometimes, however, determining the number of the subject is not easy. The problems arise in the third person singular and plural (see the conjugation section in Appendix Four) because of the -s attached to the third person singular. There are about fifteen rules to consider:

    1. Singular subjects take singular verbs:
       <u>Lisen Connery</u> *has* promised to write a paragraph for this book.
       <u>Amy Tamborlane Steffen</u> *runs* three miles every day.

    2. Singular subjects joined by *and* usually take a plural verb:
       <u>Mitchel Syp and Lisen Connery</u> *write* a column for an independent newspaper.

<u>Breakfast, lunch, and dinner</u> *have been* Shauna
Fitzgerald's favorite meals since she was two.

but

<u>Apple pie and blue cheese</u> *is* Al Davenport's favorite
dessert (because the pie and cheese is considered a
unit).

3. Plural subjects take plural verbs:
<u>Bonnie S. Davenport and Brenda E. Davenport</u>
sometimes *go* on shopping sprees for three weeks at
a time.
<u>Working crossword puzzles and writing poetry</u> have
occupied Gerry Degenhardt for years.

4. For subjects joined by *or* (or *nor*), the number of the
verb is determined by the subject closest to the verb:
Neither Charlotte Rose Davenport nor <u>Madeline E.
Davenport</u> *likes* the swing set that Grandfather Al
bought them.
Either Nancy Elizabeth Reynolds Rose or the other
<u>waitresses</u> at Lynch's Tap Room and Grill *serve* at a
moment's notice.
Either several wild cats or one huge tame <u>one</u>
scratches the cellar door nightly.

5. The subject and verb agreement is not affected by
intervening phrases:
<u>Ronald Andrew Paffrath</u>, along with several other
Madison residents, *swims* the Hammonasset River
every year.
<u>Lighthouses</u>, especial the one at the Gut near Ori-
ent Point, *send* Mary Grace Donahue Paffrath into a
dither.

6. "Be" verbs separating the subject and the predicate noun (or pronoun) agree with the subject:

    The <u>highlight</u> of Simon Etzel's return to Madison *was* the visits to his old friends.

    The <u>problem</u> with the Mets in 2004 *was* they could not hit, they could not pitch well, and they could not win the close games.

    The <u>mazes</u> of paperwork in writing a book *dazzle* the beginning writer.

7. Words that appear singular, those that do not end in –s and designate many, take a plural verb (*cattle, people, children, fish*).

    The <u>fish</u> at Southwest Reef off Clinton, Connecticut, *elude* rookie fishermen.

    The <u>police</u> *are* investigating the break-in of the local high school.

8. Some words ending in –s are plural looking but still are singular (*acoustics, athletics, politics, aerodynamics, news*):

    <u>Politics</u> in any year *is* considered volatile.

    <u>Gymnastics</u> *takes* concentration, motivation, and athletic ability.

9. Many indefinite pronouns (those that refer to no one or nothing in particular) are singular, a few are plural, and some can be singular or plural depending on the phrase that follows them (for a complete list of the three categories, see Appendix One):

    Singular: When Bill Gashlin was a big shot in business, he would tell his employees that <u>everything</u> *is* in its place or else.

Tom Beckett, Director of Athletics, Physical Education, and Recreation at Yale, told his coaches that <u>no one</u> *was* allowed in the gym after hours.

Plural: <u>Both</u> of Douglas E. Walker's boats *were* safe during the recent storm.

<u>Several</u> of Barbara Ann Walker's friends *were* winning thousands at Foxwoods when it was raided.

Singular or plural: Scott Edward Emanuelson thought that <u>most</u> of the grass *was* not worth mowing. (singular because of "grass")

Kristen Lanelle Emanuelson thinks that <u>most</u> of the boaters on the docks of Free Spirit Marine *are* intelligent, brave, and kind. (plural because of "boaters")

10. Inverted sentence order sometimes makes agreement difficult. Find the subject of the sentence and go from there (subjects are underlined):

    In the Zodiak with no life jackets *were* <u>Bradd Evans Walker</u>, <u>Seth Douglas Walker</u>, and <u>Sarah Catherine Walker</u>.

    In the back room of a dimly lit tavern *was* <u>Frank D. Scharf</u> talking with one of his clients.

11. *There is, there are, here is,* and *here are* are not the subject and verb of the sentence. The subject will follow the verb almost immediately and determines the *is* or *are*:

    There *are* several <u>talents</u> that Don Scharf has, but no one seems to know what they are.

    Here *is* <u>Ann Leyshon Fink</u> sitting at her favorite watering hole drinking a green martini.

12. Kinds of measurement usually take singular verbs (length, height, time, space, and so on):
    <u>Five hundred dollars</u> *was* the prize John Cumisky won for the ice fishing contest.
    Dan Fitzgerald thought that <u>three hundred years</u> *was* a long time to wait for the Red Sox to win a championship.

13. *Who, whom, which,* and *that* can be singular or plural depending on the word to which each refers:
    <u>People</u> who *do* not know Peter James Butler *are* surprised when they find out about his fishing prowess (plural verb because of "people").
    Howard Adolph George Greim, <u>one</u> of those helpers who *gives* of himself unselfishly, wants no praise for his kindness.
    Marion Edith Greim enjoys watching <u>athletes</u> who *give* their all.

14. In certain cases, two words (or sometimes three or four) joined by *and* take a singular verb:
    <u>Law and order</u> *was* a must for a frontier town just beginning to function.
    <u>Pomp and circumstance</u> *identifies* those parties that rate as galas.

15. Special considerations: There are certain words like *jury, committee, gaggle,* and *panel* that are singular if the action of the group is unanimous or plural if the group is acting not as a unit but as individuals:
    The <u>jury</u> *have* decided that it would be better to postpone their decisions until they can come to a conclusion. (The jury act as individuals.)

The <u>panel</u> *has* concluded that the expansion of the Griswold airport into condominium plots would be a detriment to the town. (The panel acts unanimously.)

AGREEMENT OF PRONOUN AND ANTECEDENT

Fundamentally, a pronoun must agree with its **antecedent** (the word to which the pronoun refers) in gender (masculine, feminine, or neuter), number (singular or plural), or case (subjective or objective). The rule sounds simple, but several variations make this rule slightly complicated.

1. Singular nouns (two or more) joined by "and" require a plural pronoun:
   Jean Elizabeth Walton and Sherrill Jean Walton like *their* drinks made only by *their* favorite bartender.
   Cats and dogs prefer *their* food in separate dishes.

2. Singular nouns joined by "or" or "nor" need a singular pronoun.
   John Philip Conte, Joseph F. Keough, or Joseph G. Murphy prepares *his* sermon carefully, with perfect English.
   A small skiff or a sixty-eight foot motor yacht requires deftness to handle *it* in rough seas.

3. A singular noun and a plural noun joined by "or" requires a pronoun to agree with the nearer word:
   Tom Schneiter or his *relatives* are famous for *their* quick wit.
   Sue Schneiter's relatives or Sue herself is famous for *her* magnificent recipes.

4. Indefinite pronouns (see Appendix One for a complete list) are sometimes singular, sometimes plural, and sometimes either depending on their use:

   Caitlin Keeton thought that *everyone* in her sewing class should provide *her* own thread.

   Both of Mickie and Tony Giordano's wallets turned up after someone had found *them* by the side of the road.

   Most of the <u>boys</u> in Elizabeth "Polly" Lott Donnellan's class in college could not control *themselves* when she entered the classroom.

   Most of the <u>field</u> lost *its* brilliance when the sun dried up both flowers and grass.

5. Company names, books, countries, and so on require singular pronouns even though the name or title may sound plural:

   According to Dick Spero, *McDonald's* treats *its* employees better than any other company.

   The Sound and the Fury rates as an American classic because *its* characters are real.

6. Collective nouns require a singular pronoun when the group is acting as a whole and a singular pronoun when the members of the group act individually:

   The *jury* deemed *its* verdict just.

   The *jury* departed for *their* homes because the judge thought the panel needed a rest.

7. Those nouns that look plural (*athletics, physics, mumps, news*) but have a singular meaning take a singular antecedent:

Physics found *its* place in public schools from the early forties on.

8. *Every* or *many a* before a single noun or a group of singular nouns needs a singular antecedent:
   Many a heart *was* broken by Vincent J. Saputo while he was growing up in the Bronx.
   Every radish, carrot, and spinach leaf never made *its* way to the table because the deer got there first.

9. *The number of* is singular and takes a singular antecedent regardless of what follows:
   The number of teachers in the Madison school system decreases *its* ranks every semester.
   A number of is plural and takes a plural antecedent.
   A number of teachers visited Hilton Head on *their* mid-winter vacation.

MISPLACED AND DANGLING MODIFIERS

Syntax requires certain placement of words to make sense. A misplaced modifer (adjective or adverb single word, phrase, or clause) sometimes causes hysterics and at other times causes the clucking of language purists. Even the word "dangling" had to be presented carefully to avoid snickers from students in the classroom who had not heard the term.

A **misplaced modifier** is an adjective or adverb that needs to be relocated in a sentence. The adverb most often misplaced is *only*. Notice that in the following sentences the placement of *only* changes the meaning of the sentence slightly:

Lorraine Saputo only eats at Lynch's. (no water, nothing except food)

Only Lorraine Saputo eats at Lynch's. (its only customer)

Lorraine Saputo eats only at Lynch's. (and no other restaurant)

Lorraine Saputo eats at Lynch's only. (emphasizes "Lynch's" and implies that restaurant is the only one)

Other modifiers that can be misplaced are single adverbs (single adjectives are difficult to misplace because they usually are placed near the noun or pronoun they modify) and participial phrases. Adjective clauses demand to be placed right after the word they modify.

Misplaced participial phrase: <u>Arriving late</u>, the teacher berated the children. (Obviously the "teacher" was not the late one—the children were.)

Corrected: The teacher berated the children <u>arriving late</u>.

Misplaced single adverb: As the hobo weaved around the house <u>drunkenly</u>, the woman inside shook with fear. (awkward)

Corrected: As the hobo weaved <u>drunkenly</u> around the house, the woman inside shook with fear. (better)

Dangling modifiers "dangle" because they do not attach themselves sensibly to the right word in the sentence. And sometimes these "danglers" can be quite humorous.

Dangling: To demand attention in the cafeteria, the children were told to line up against the wall.

Corrected: To demand attention in the cafeteria, the teachers told the children to line up against the wall.

Dangling: Dressed in sequins and pearls, the dog chased the lady into an alley.

Corrected: Into an alley, the dog chased the lady dressed in sequins and pearls.

PLACEMENT OF PARTS OF SPEECH

Nouns

Nouns, since they function five ways (subject, direct object, indirect object, object of the preposition, and predicate noun), set up anywhere they make sense. The usual placement depends on the use, of course, but even with certain usage, positioning might differ.

For example, nouns as <u>subjects</u> usually come before the *verb*. (<u>Spencer Lockhart</u> *reads* ten books a week. <u>Peyton Patterson</u> *lives* next to the Lockharts.) However, in certain situations, the subject can come after the verb. (There *is* <u>Pat Williams</u> working in the yard. Why *was* <u>Don Williams</u> inside watching television?)

Adjectives

Writers place <u>adjectives</u> three ways: Before the noun, after the noun, and after a linking or "be" verb. (See Appendix Three for a list of these verbs and other helping verbs.)

Before the *noun*: <u>tourist</u> *destination*; <u>fishing</u> *expo*; <u>camera</u> equipment

After the *noun* (usually in pairs): *Patriots,* <u>cool</u> and <u>determined</u>; *illusion,* <u>baffling</u> and <u>spectacular</u>; *Mount Etna,* <u>threatening</u> and <u>protective</u>

After a linking *verb*: Caroline Fitzgerald said that Nana's spaghetti *tasted* <u>awful</u>.

Danny Fitzgerald *stayed* <u>calm</u> as he reeled in the giant striper.

"Big" Dan Fitzgerald *grew* <u>agitated</u> as the Celtics dropped to last place.

After a "be" verb as the main *verb*:

Jackie Catania *is* <u>best</u> at Sicilian cuisine.

Kathy Lynch *was* <u>successful</u> in every real estate transaction last year.

K. C. Sweitzer *has been* <u>good</u> at checkers since he was three.

<u>Adjective phrases</u> and <u>clauses</u> usually are placed next to the *words* they modify.

Prepositional phrase: The *young man* <u>in the back</u> <u>of the bus</u> missed his stop.

<u>On the phone</u> for an hour, *Jennifer Catania* convinced the tax collector that a mistake had been made.

Participial phrase: <u>Barking like a seal</u>, *Leo Fitzgerald* drew *attention* <u>to himself</u> in church.

Michael George Rollinson, <u>expecting the motorist to cooperate</u>, shook his *head* <u>in disbelief</u> when the driver lied.

Adverbs

<u>Single word adverbs</u> should be placed as near the *words* they modify as possible. Some words like *only* (see above), depending on its position in the sentence, change the meaning of the sentence. For example, years ago our town instituted a softball league with two divisions with a rule that read, "A player may only play for one division." After playing two games in both divisions, I was asked why I was breaking the rules. I said I wasn't. I was <u>only playing</u>. The rule was changed to read, "A player may participate in one division only."

> **Single word adverbs:** Nancy O'Shea Bennett <u>ambitiously</u> *opened* a store at a ski resort in Vermont.
>
> Dean Bennett, Jr., <u>systematically</u> *checks* Ebay for deals on used cars.

<u>Adverb clauses</u> and <u>phrases</u> follow the rule above, with the possible exception that an adverb clause sometimes may be placed anywhere in the sentence without affecting meaning because the modification is clear.

> **Phrases:** When Dennis Randall *was approached* <u>by the "gladiator"</u> (phrase) near the Coliseum in Rome, the smelly Roman impostor insisted on posing for a picture.
>
> As Donna Randall *was sauntering* <u>down Duval Street</u> (phrase) in Key West, she drew stares from the locals.

Notice that these adverb phrases must be quite close to the words they modify; in the examples of clauses, however, notice that the adverb clause can be placed anywhere in the sentence usually without changing the meaning.

> **Clauses:** <u>While Corey Nilson was reeling in the fifty-pound bass</u>, he *paused* so that his family could take pictures.

Corey Nilson, <u>while he was reeling in the fifty-pound bass</u>, *paused* so that his family could take pictures.

Corey Nilson *paused* so that his family could take pictures <u>while he was reeling in the fifty-pound bass</u>.

The other parts of speech are self-explanatory. Conjunctions, for example, must connect two or more items and must be placed between at least two sentence parts. Interjections come anywhere—usually in some sort of dialogue.

SENTENCE VARIETY

Nothing causes tedium as much as reading consecutive sentences that begin with the subject and immediately follow with a verb. To vary syntax, good writers start sentences in many ways:

- Begin with a single word adjective: <u>Famished</u>, Timothy Barry took time out from managing The Jonathan Edwards Vineyard in Stonington, Connecticut, and ate a sandwich bought from George Peter Papadopoulus.

- Begin with two or more adjectives: <u>Driven, personable, and vivacious</u>, Joanie Howard works diligently at the *New Haven Register*.

- Begin with a single adverb: <u>Proudly</u>, Joanne Howard's mother brags about her daughter's work.

- Begin with two or more adverbs: <u>Coolly, precisely, and deftly</u>, Danny Jones performs magic in the kitchen.

- Begin with a participle: <u>Approving</u>, Collette and Judy Sembler nodded at the decision made by the coach.

- Begin with a participial phrase: <u>Fighting ten-foot waves,</u> Captain Chris Banack drove his Grady White into the teeth of the storm.

- Begin with an appositive: <u>Salesperson of the year for the last three years,</u> Shari Murphy Slight avers that Seasilver contains everything beneficial known to man.

- Begin with an infinitive phrase: <u>To make her music even more beautiful,</u> Bonnie Leigh Murphy took her amplifiers away.

- Begin with a noun clause: <u>Whoever partakes of libations at Celtica Public House in Newport, Rhode Island,</u> will inevitably meet Mark and Gina Brennan, the owners, and Jenni Jones, the ultimate bartender.

- Begin with an adverb clause: <u>Whenever Jane Marie Curiha and Jane Thayer Brodbar get together,</u> serious conversation ensues.

- Begin with a single direct object: <u>Washington, D.C.,</u> Courtney Fellows Cotter loves.

- Begin with a gerund phrase: <u>Working diligently</u> Bill Cotter espouses. <u>Sitting around</u> in the Key West sun was Kevin Walsh's dream.

- Begin with a noun clause used as a direct object: <u>Whatever was lost in the fire</u> Samantha Lynn Witkowski claimed as personal loss.

- Begin with a noun clause as the subject: <u>Whenever the sun rose</u> began Brenda Walsh's trip around Middle Beach Road.

- Begin with an appositive phrase: <u>Both a lover of fine music and a creator of fine foods,</u> Peter George "Pano" Papadopoulus whistles while he cooks.

Using the above suggestions, write a few sentences, but vary the beginnings. You will find that writing is not only fun but rewarding—even though you might be writing just for yourself. If you e-mail a bunch, try the variety there.

If, then, variety is the spice of life, variety is definitely the spice of writing.

COORDINATION AND/OR SUBORDINATION

A huge part of a writer's syntax , along with parallel structure, is weighing larger elements of sentences and either balancing them or making one more important than the other. Knowing how to coordinate and subordinate also aids in reading texts, especially when the teacher or boss says, "Pick out the salient points and be ready for the testing/selling."

Coordination occurs with simple sentences joined by coordinating conjunctions (*and, but, or, nor, for, yet*) or correlative conjunctions (*either . . . or, neither . . . nor, both . . . and, not only . . . but (also), whether . . . or*). See the compound sentences below.

Subordination happens when a simple sentence is changed by adding a subordinating conjunction (*as, because, since, after, although, even though, that, so that, if, when,* etc.). While coordination implies that the sentences joined are equal in importance, subordination implies that the sentence subordinated is less important than the main sentence. The author hints that what is subordinated is nice being there and may add something to the text; however, it is merely a detail. (See discussion of complex and compound/complex sentences below.)

Sentences can vary even further with craft because there are four types of sentences, which we will discuss first: the simple sentence, the compound sentence, the complex sentence, and the compound/complex sentence.

Simple Sentence

Even simple sentences can vary because of the arrangement of words, but basically a simple sentence contains a verb (or a series of verbs) and a subject (or many subjects). The shortest simple sentence? **Go!** (imperative "go" and the implied subject "you")

> **One *verb,* one <u>subject</u>:** <u>Laurie Nettleton Watson</u> *attends* every reunion of her class.

> **A *series of verbs,* one <u>subject</u>:** Mimi Ford Adkins *runs* marathons, *cleans* attics, and *tells* the best jokes.

> **A *series of verbs* with <u>many subjects</u>:** <u>Walter Charles Welsh</u>, <u>Elizabeth Weaver Welsh</u>, and <u>Kevin William Welsh</u> *read* books, *take* hikes, and *sleep* late.

Compound Sentence

The compound sentence is nothing more than two or more simple sentences punctuated correctly. The reason writers "string" these together is that each unit has a close connection to the other. This connection is the exclusive job of a coordinating conjunction (*and, but, or, nor, for, yet*); also, the following words can be used to make the connection obvious: *however, thus, consequently, subsequently, moreover, more importantly.* For a more complete list of transitional expressions, see Appendix Two.

Notice the following sentence: Erin Smith celebrated the most glorious wedding ever seen at the Surf Club; moreover, several magazines covered the event.

Typical compound sentence: <u>Steven Michael "Boz" Adkins establishes moorings for local boaters</u>, but <u>he himself does not fish, boat, or swim</u>.

Not so typical compound sentence: <u>Harvey Brandon catches tautog better than anyone else</u>, <u>his son is the favorite of every teacher in the school</u>, and <u>his wife cooks the best of anyone in the neighborhood</u>.

Complex Sentence

The complex sentence sounds intricate but really has only two parts, <u>one simple sentence</u> and at least one (or more) *subordinate clause(s)*.

> **One <u>simple sentence</u>, one *subordinate clause*:** *As Greg Doonan sits quietly with calculator and pencil,* <u>he figures the price of a house based on present standards</u>.

> **One <u>simple sentence</u>, many *subordinate clauses*:** <u>Gee Collins presides in most conversations</u> *because he is uncannily brilliant, because people listen to his cogency, and because his knowledge surpasses everyone else's.*

Compound/Complex Sentence

This type could get complicated but basically comprises two (or more) <u>simple sentences</u> and one (or more) *subordinate clause(s)*.

I'll let Ole Edvart Rolvaag, from his *Giants in the Earth,* present the first example:

> *Before the Germans in the morning,* <u>they came to examine Per Hansa's house</u>; <u>Tonseten had told them of one of his neighbours</u> *who had built a dwelling and stable under one roof;*

<u>they thought</u> *it would be well worth the trouble to go and look at a structure of that kind;* <u>they themselves were just beginning, and needed ideas</u>.

And Herman Melville from *Moby Dick*:

> <u>You observe</u> *that in the ordinary swimming position of the Sperm Whale, the front of his head presents an almost wholly vertical plane to the water;* <u>you observe</u> *that the lower part of that front slopes considerably backwards,* so as to furnish more of a retreat for the long socket *which receives the boom-like lower jaw;* <u>you observe</u> *that the mouth is entirely under the head,* much in the same way, indeed, *as though your mouth were entirely under your chin.*

And last, but I presume not least, from Dan Mulvey:

> <u>The Key West Harbor Walk</u>, *which takes the average tourist three days to complete,* <u>starts in the middle or at either end</u>; <u>diversions take over</u>, and <u>the casual walker tries snapping pictures of the huge bread-eating tarpon fed by children</u>, *while street vendors catch your attention even though their jewelry will turn your finger or neck green,* and <u>iguanas lead their masters on leashes</u> *as they both head for Schooner's and a Bud.*

Syntax, then, must dominate the thoughts of all writers, who must convey to their readers exact thoughts. Raymond Carver once told an audience that it was not unusual for him to spend weeks choosing a correct word, and his poetry and short stories reflect that care. Of course, married to Tess Gallagher, an extraordinary wordsmith in her own right, Carver had his own in-house critic.

Ready to write some paragraphs? Chapter Four is loaded with paragraph plans.

Writing, when properly managed
(as you may be sure I think mine is)
is but a different name for conversation.

Lawrence Stern

Chapter Four

DEVELOPING PARAGRAPHS FOR PARTICULAR PURPOSES

From *Merriam-Webster's Collegiate Dictionary*, Eleventh Edition:

> **par·a·graph** n. a subdivision of a written composition that consists of one or more sentences, deals with one point or gives the words of one speaker, and begins on a new usu. indented line

A loose definition, to be sure, but enough to start with. The shortest paragraph, then, would be "Go!" and the longest is anybody's guess. Somewhere in between exists the perfect paragraph that anyone is capable of constructing.

To start with, a writer should have some inkling about the purpose, subject matter, **tone** (the attitude the writer wants the reader to understand), plan, and arrangements of details before the pen(cil) hits the paper. If bosses of companies wish to inform their workers about lateness, for example, the purpose and subject matter are clear, the tone more than likely serious, and the message brief and to the point. If a teacher wishes to poke fun with an in-house letter at certain events in the school building or district, the tone might be lighthearted (to make a point), the arrangement of details would list the "killer barb" last, and language that administrations use (*prioritize, bottom line, accountability, behavioral objectives*), satirized.

Purpose varies. Does the writer want to instruct, inform, persuade, or simply entertain? For example, here is an informational paragraph written by a former student who now is flying jet planes for the Navy. I asked her what process she had to go through to become a pilot. Stephanie Gay responded with the following (with **transitional expressions** in boldface):

The United States Naval Flight training is an intense evolution. **After** graduating from the United States Naval Academy, a Naval Reserve Officer Training Corps, or Officer Candidate School, all pilots report to Naval Air Station, Pensacola, Florida. It is here that the syllabus begins. **Initially**, all student naval aviators endure six weeks of basic aviation classes, as well as physical tests. **After** completion of this course, all students enter a T-34C Mentor squadron. Whether in Naval Air Station, Whiting, Florida, or in Corpus Christi, Texas, all pilots undergo the same flight training. Each pilot flies multiple familiarization, aerobatic forms, and radio instrument flights. It is this phase where the fun begins. Learning how to fly is rewarding as well as frustrating at times, and many students will come back from a flight elated because it has gone well; on other days, students look as though they are ready to punch someone. **After this phase**, pilots select which pipeline they wish to enter. Some fly helicopters while others fly jets or propeller aircraft. No matter what they fly, getting "winged" is the ultimate goal. Having fulfilled a dream, every pilot, no matter how difficult the training was, rejoices on this day.

Another former student, Matt DeCapua, an aspiring actor in New York City, always had a gift of humor in his writing. The tone in the following paragraph is obvious:

Upon learning that I live in a New York apartment with three female roommates, all my male friends share the same reaction: a somewhat prurient leer and a variation of "Oh, *really*! What's that like?" I am endlessly amused by the automatic assumption that my living arrangement is a 24-hour orgy. The reality includes catfights, emotional roller coasters,

and a cascade of feminine hygiene products should I accidentally contact any surface in the shower. Were I ever actually
to become physically entangled with one of my surrogate sis-
ters, an irreparable and catastrophic end to harmony would
inevitably ensue. And while they are all quite appealing, I
think of other things because affordable housing in this city is
harder to find than you might think.

In high school, he shone with brilliance, humor, and wide-
spread popularity. Remember the name: Matt DeCapua will be
famous some day soon.

PARAGRAPH DEVELOPMENT

Building a house? If the answer is "Yes," then you do not start nailing boards together willy-nilly. The first step begins with an idea
and then blossoms with an architect's rendition of that idea. The
order of the plan outlines the size and arrangement of rooms,
which may change as the building progresses. The décor depends
largely on the taste of the owner, but certainly there is careful
attention given to colors, types of wood, pieces of furniture, etc.,
and how these things blend together with thought toward the
transition from one room to another. The finished product results
from much discussion and thought, and for the owner, the house
that finally stands tall becomes the first dream house. However, as
the saying goes, one has to build three houses to reach perfection.
Back to the drawing/revision board.

Building a paragraph is much the same. The writer starts with
an idea, the type of "subject matter" (house), proceeds with the
plan of development, carefully arranges details so that certain
emphases happen, and edits the work to make sure the grammar,

syntax, spelling, vocabulary, and subject matter measure up to specifications, just as the house measures up to the blueprints. To finish off the dream paragraph, the writer carefully chooses **transitional expressions** (in boldface below, there are a few suggestions next to each plan and arrangement of details)—the rugs, the carpets, the paints—to guide the reader from one sentence (or room) to another and from one paragraph, or page, or chapter to another. A more complete scheme of these transitional expressions is referenced in Appendix Two.

Paragraphs develop according to plans, and at the risk of stating the obvious, here are the ones I used to give my students: A paragraph can be developed by (Notice, purists, no colon after "by.")

- **An anecdote.** The entire paragraph contains a beginning, a middle, and an end. It might be amusing—what some call a locality story (You had to be there!)—or it could be downright funny, but it is a unit unto itself. **(after a while, soon, previously)**

> Children are funny creatures. Melissa, a fellow actor in *Noises Off!* has her daughter with her at rehearsal tonight. Isabella approaches us while we talk and asks us whether or not we know that people live in the city dump. "*Really?*" Melissa asks, **while** giving me a look (you know the look—the *what now?* look). Isabella nods solemnly and goes on to tell us that she has seen people eating out of trash bins, which must mean they live in the dump. "Really," Melissa says **again** and raises an eyebrow. But **before** she can continue, Isabella interrupts and tells us she has been sending them letters. But she doesn't send them in the mail like regular letters. No, she sends them by putting them in the trash bin in her kitchen. She **then** scurries back to her bag to show us an example. It's written in a large, childish hand with sparkly markers as the

medium. We squint at the crumpled missive that reads, "Dear people at the dump, I hope you've been getting my letters. I'm going to put some food in this one when I get home. Please drink your water because you can die without it. Love, Isabella." Melissa and I can barely contain ourselves **at this point**. We're sniggering behind our hands at the innocence and brilliance of this child. "This is very nice, Isabella. But there are other ways to help the, um, the dump people. We could go to a special kitchen and help feed them. Would you like that?" Isabella looks at us searchingly and then nods. "But," she states, hand raised, "only if I can draw pictures for them." Melissa can contain herself **no longer** and, laughing, tells her that pictures would be quite nice, indeed.

Written by Amy Jirsa, former student of the author. She is an aspiring actress for both stage and screen, teaches drama to small groups, and has starred in a few productions out of Nebraska. At the Class of '95 reunion of Daniel Hand High School, Amy was the star.

- **An incident.** Again, this type of paragraph has a beginning, middle, and end, but the tone is serious with very little attempt at humor. **(immediately, later, today, first, then, next)**

    Watching a tuna prepared for shipping to Japan highlights visits to Montauk, New York. **First**, the blue fin (300 pounds or better constitutes a giant) is hoisted by the tail, eviscerated, and finned (the dorsal and bottom fins removed by what looks like a chainsaw). **Then**, a Japanese tuna expert inserts a tube into specific areas of the fish, extracts a tube of meat, smells it, tastes it, and determines the quality. **Next**, the expert decides the weight and the price, lowers the body to the ground, and detaches the tail, which is weighed separately and that weight is subtracted from the original weigh-in. **Finally,** the tuna "coffin," that huge fiberglass tub, is partially filled with ice, the carcass placed in the coffin, then filled to the top with ice, and, with the lid secured, the parcel is ready to be shipped to Japan, where it will arrive in fewer than twenty-four hours.

Dr. Thomas Suchanek, a noted paleontologist and former student (Durham High School, Class of '65), wrote the following (used with his permission):

A dive to the deep-sea ranks as an experience that can bend one's mind and etch lifetime memories. **Getting there** was part of a detective story that led me to dive 12,000 feet deep into the Caribbean Sea. I was studying sea grasses that grow in the shallow lagoons of St. Croix in the U.S. Virgin Islands. Winter storms, especially hurricanes, often create, in addition to other types of more familiar destruction, monstrous waves that tear up sea grass beds, transporting the seagrasses down steep slopes and across abysmal plains. Tiny blades of grass (with strange names like *Thalassia* and

Syringodium), no bigger than 1/16th of an inch in diameter and several inches long, can take nearly three years to tumble down into the deep sea. Once landing at the bottom, they are carried along by currents and are so widely distributed that there may be 30–50 feet between individual blades.

On the surface, sea urchins gobble up sea grass blades at every opportunity. But the big question was: Who can take advantage of this food source in the crushing pressure zone of 400 atmospheres (6000 pounds per square inch), near zero degree, jet-black darkness of the abysmal zone?

To answer this question, I used the Woods Hole Oceanographic Institution's research submersible "ALVIN," a self-propelled submarine with mechanical arms for grasping deep-sea animals, plants, and sediments, a large rear mounted propeller, a set of enormous flood lights, and a 1500-pound battery pack to drive it all. A titanium sphere with a 6-foot inside diameter and with three 8-inch-thick portholes holds two scientists and a pilot, plus radio equipment and a couple of coffee cans (the reader can guess what they were for).

When I signed up for this cruise, ALVIN had been in the refurbish shop, getting certified to 12,000 feet from its previous dive limit of 10,000. I was then placed on the "maiden voyage" to 12,000 feet, an honor I wasn't exactly sure I wanted, because all I could think of was the movie "Das Boot." The dive day in that movie started at 0600 hours—all hands on deck, preparing to launch the sub from the mother ship LULU. The dive there resembled a launch from the Kennedy Space Center, all systems checked and double-checked.

We were briefed on **ALVIN's** safety features, including what would happen if the sub gets tangled at a huge depth and can't surface. **First**, each mechanical arm had explosive joints that could be blown off to release the tangled sub. If that procedure didn't work, the 1500-pound battery pack could be released. **As a last resort**, we were shown a key in a small cabinet, which fit into a hole in the floor of the sub. If I turned the key 90 degrees counter-clockwise, the titanium sphere would be released from the sub, launching it, because of its inherent buoyancy, toward the surface at some unimaginable speed.

It took **8 hours** to descend 12,000 feet Below 300 feet everything was pitch-black, except for the sparks of light igniting from the bioluminescent organisms touching the sub (or its bow wake) as it sank into the depths. Floodlights were kept off to preserve battery power. Worms, jellyfish, fin fish, and clouds of amorphous bacteria-laden gelatinous blobs of "marine snow" lit up each port. **Once at the bottom**, the lights came on and we cruised for several hours photographing and collecting sea grass blades—being eaten by deep-sea urchins.

We collected the urchins too and conducted tissue analyses to prove that the sea grasses were the carbon sources from which the urchins were deriving their primary source of nutrition. **All in all**, this experience proved exciting and fruitful because I observed places in the deep that no human had ever laid eyes on before and added just a smidgen of scientific understanding to our knowledge of the deep sea.

Tom is currently Research Manager for the U.S. Geological Survey—Biologica, Research Discipline.

- **Description or definition of a person, place, thing, idea, or quality.** Both "description" and "definition" can be loosely combined into one category, but my thought is that accuracy depends on the exact thought before attempting the paragraph.

By describing something, the writer does, however, define it. **(as an illustration, for this purpose)**

The State of Connecticut recognized Kaili Floyd of Branford for the following paragraph; she was ten, at the time, and in the fourth grade.

> Do you like the beach? Do you like the park? Do you like the sounds of children playing? Owenego is the best place. The first reason is that there is a park containing baby swings, big kid swings, bars to climb, two slides, a basketball court, a tennis court, and space to run around. The second reason is the beach. Although the beach is crowded on sunny days, some bathers prefer to sit on the grass, others enjoy jumping from the raft fifty feet off shore, and still others wander the shore, collecting shells. The final reason: The sound of young and old swimming and the sound of the waves crashing onto the sand lull you to sleep. I recommend Owenego for great family fun.

or

I once wrote a piece, my first attempt at fiction, for Caroline Nuzzi who at that time was the editor of *Heading Out*, a hand-out magazine with features on the outdoors. Here is another "Fishing Buddy."

> Ralph, Ronnie, Pete (two of them), Jack, Gerald, Quippy, Doug, Bobby, Frank, Sue, or Shauna—by any other name still a fishing buddy. (S)he, willing to fish on a minute's notice, forgets items that I eventually supply, complains when the stripers don't hit immediately, constantly suggests we move to another spot, and swears mightily after losing a big one. Garrulous, crapulous, and naïve, (s)he will offer Sister Gail a beer at six-thirty in the morning, Father Chuck a shot of tequila at

seven, bring just enough beer for self-consumption, and criticize the lack of beverages aboard. Pointing out things along the way like "Look! An offspray! (meaning osprey)" or "Stripers hit only at night! (as we reel one in at 12 noon)" or "You should have an automatic wench for the anchor (and then, what would my wife say?)" or, pointing to a vessel several miles away, "That's a Luhrs, 35 footer, with twin 300 Cats." (It was really Falkner Island off Guilford, Connecticut, but if one stretched imagination, it might have been a vessel). (S)he will wax smug, let out an orgiastic scream at landing a fish, pose informative, act scholarly, and exude self-importance all at once, but humbly accept the compliments forthcoming. (S)he's my fishing buddy.

- **Comparison.** This type of paragraph compares two like or unlike items. The emphasis is on comparison rather than on contrast. **(also, in the same manner, both, like)**

    Sicilians call Mount Etna "Big Mother" for several reasons. **Like** the Italian matriarch, she nourishes the surrounding territories with rich soil that feeds her "children" nourishing olives, almonds, grapes, oranges, and lemons. Cabbages, cauliflower, onions, garlic, tomatoes, lettuce, and all sorts of other vegetables grow to huge proportions, while contented grazing animals furnish meat that is lean and tasty. **Furthermore**, if the "children" act up and become obstreperous, Big Mother keeps them in check by wiping out houses, sometimes even small and large communities. **Always** she reminds them with playful pats on the rear end that she is in control. **At night**, just before everyone is tucked into bed, on her side like an apron she displays her beautiful deep red fire in the shape of a valentine, a Christmas tree, an Easter egg, a clown, a soul returning from the dead to give presents, or even an angel to remind her brood she is always there.

> Written by the author after a trip to Sicily where,
> in Palermo, the waiters respond to the question
> "Do you speak English?" with "No—Italian"

- **Contrast.** If the writer wishes to show just differences between similar or dissimilar items, then this is the paragraph plan to incorporate. (**on the other hand, yet, but**)

> The differences in the poetry of Emily Dickinson and Edwin Arlington Robinson remind me of the differences between night and day. **While** Dickinson's images of nature ("a slender fellow in the grass") might seem playful, Robinson's on the other hand reek of depression (the leaves "Now and then / They stopped, and stayed there—just to let . . . know / How dead they were"). If Dickinson speaks of **love**, the lines resonate with positive thought ("Love—is . . . The Exponent of Earth"); Robinson rarely speaks of anything except **hate** ("he took the draught / Of bitterness himself"), and the lines sometimes cause revulsion ("And Richard Corey, one calm summer night / Went home and put a bullet in his head"). Further, almost all of Dickinson's poetry contains **erratic meter** while Robinson's is nearly all **iambic pentameter**. The rhyme is **consistent** with Robinson (light-night; me-sea; paid-made), but Dickinson **plays** with our ears with off rhyme (come-nun; one-known; despair-here). Robinson's collection of "Children of the Night" stands in stark contrast to the image of Emily Dickinson, dressed in white, absorbing the things of nature, love, and communication. **In conclusion,**

both these famous American poets might be considered typical because they tried to reflect the circumstances of their individual lives.

- **Comparison/contrast.** This plan gives the writer a wide approach to any two items. I would warn students not to write about water skiing and snow skiing because after reading three thousand paragraphs on that topic I had had enough. **(like, on the contrary)**

Here is an example of a comparison/contrast paragraph written by a former student, Lisen Connery, one of the few students I know who volunteered to read *An American Tragedy* by Theodore Dreiser during her April vacation.

On Holidays

I personally prefer **Thanksgiving**, such a comfortable holiday based simply on a sumptuous spread of food and the idea that we should be grateful for all we have. **Christmas**, of course, involves a similarly elaborate traditional meal, but there seems to be more to think about: the buildup of cocktail parties, formal suppers, informal ice-skating dates, and tree-lighting viewings, not to mention the pressures of finding the perfect gift for each person on the ever-growing list coupled with the not-so-growing bank account. On **Thanksgiving**, gifts, if even necessary, involve nothing more than a bag of chocolates or a bouquet of orange and red flowers. On this holiday, perfectly acceptable attire might comprise a sweater and pants or even a cozy jumper accented with bright tights. **Christmas** outfits range from tiny black dresses to fit over noticeably round holiday bellies to festive reindeer sweaters to sequined cardigans that are holidayish without being garish. **Both these holidays**, however, have one thing in common: loving one's friends and family and neighbors; each holiday reminds us of the importance of charity and the strength of goodwill.

- **Argument (or opinion).** Sometimes, especially in the op-ed pages, writers argue for or against topics or express their opinions on issues current. **(to repeat, in fact)**

The following paragraphs, written by Emily Jirsa, Hand High School Class of '97, show the benefits of being a twin:

> I have a valid **reason** for sometimes lacking independence: I am a twin; I have been codependent since birth. Often I find myself spewing the words, "Do you want to come with me? I don't want to go alone!" However, this lack of independence costs little, for being a twin equals a gift. **For example**, instead of learning how to share in preschool or with another sibling at age two or three, the meaning of sharing I learned in the womb, which, although I do not recall those nine months of close quarters, I hear is quite small.
>
> **To display further** the benefits of being a dyad, I'll do a little contrasting. Not once, in all my elhi years, was I subjected to that terrifying first day of school alone. **Whereas** most non-twins travel that long road to school in solitude, my companion accompanied me and even saved me a seat on the bus for the weary ride home. **Furthermore**, that nerve-racking, anxiety-raising experience of going for the driver's license eased significantly because my best friend was there too. And birthdays? **Although** I have no idea what it is like to have a day all to myself, I do know twice as much cake, twice as many invited friends, twice as many presents, and twice as much fun.

- **Cause and effect.** History texts and biographies are jammed with these types. **(as a result, for these reasons)**

Adversity often gave [Ralph Waldo] Emerson a strange elation. All through this spring and summer [of 1837] he was living on the stretch; he had frequent moments of almost visionary intensity. The end of April witnessed one such quick updraft of Emerson's spirits. He was reading Goethe's translation of Plotinus on art. Plotinus wants us to see the artistry behind and shaping the artifact. Emerson gives the idea sudden life by saying the art of shipbuilding is "all of the ship but the wood." As artistry is more important than artifact, so, Emerson now concludes, "character is higher than intellect."

From *Emerson: The Mind on Fire* by Robert D. Richardson Jr.

or

Events on the national scene in early 1850 jarred him [Walt Whitman] back into political action. The acquisition of some 850,000 square miles of land in the southwest and the population explosion in California in the wake of the gold rush made the issue of slavery in the territories tense once more. A seeming solution to the problem appeared in the compromise measures forged by the Southern Whig senator Henry Clay and endorsed by his fellow Whig from Massachusetts Daniel Webster. According to the compromise, California would be admitted to the Union a free state, but there would be no legal restrictions on slavery in Utah and New Mexico, where, Webster rationalized, the climate was not salubrious to slavery anyway. To satisfy the south, a stringent fugitive slave law would be enforced by which recaptured slaves would not be allowed jury trial and those who aided them would be subject to a thousand-dollar fine or six months in jail. Southerners and conservative Northerners were, in general, pleased with the compromise. But fierce complaints came from both sides, especially Northern anti-slavery activists who hated the fugitive slave law.

From *Walt Whitman's America* by David S. Reynolds

- **Facts and examples.** This plan, almost never by itself, helps other plans work. One cannot, for example, write a paragraph with a plan of cause and effect without using facts or examples. (**to illustrate, a case in point**)

> Connie [Mack] was back with Hartford **in 1886**; and that season the Connecticut capital was taken into the Eastern League. It was a pretty snug compact loop, and included Newark, Jersey City, Bridgeport, Waterbury, and Meriden. Connie's pay was advanced to $200 a month, and in East Brookfield they were looking on the McGillicuddys as pluto-crats. That was impressive money! Mack **continued** to catch Frank Gilmore in all his games. He also helped out at first base when Billy Kreig caught. However, his **1886** batting average of .248 for 69 Eastern League games was scarcely enough to have big-league owners camping on his doorstep.

> *Connie Mack* by Fred Lieb (inscribed by Lieb to my father, Daniel F. X. Mulvey, who at that time was the Sports Editor for *The New Haven Register*)

- **Combination.** Of course, this idea of planning pervades most paragraphs. When one comes right down to it, writing a para-graph *without* a combination of plans is nearly impossible, like trying to write the Great American Novel on the *point* of a pin (thank you, John Irving). The following paragraph proves this point:

Substitute teaching ranks in the top five of America's worst jobs, and the other four don't count. **First**, the students arm themselves *against* the substitute teacher. Their spitballs in place, the excuses to leave the room ready, and esoteric signals practiced, the hooligans wait in ambush. **Second**, the teacher-substituted-for has failed to include today's schedule; instead, the schedule included is only for emergency evacuation procedures after Period Two. **Third**, the substitute teacher is left with a rank book that was last year's. The only comforting thought for the sub is that the salary received for a day's work will not even pay to fill a half full gas tank.

Written by the author, who vowed never to return to the classroom as a substitute teacher

Now that the subject matter and the plan(s) are in place, the arrangement of the rooms, the details, places upon this builder another set of structures. How does the writer arrange details that the reader will understand immediately? I narrow them to four with an introduction to transitional terms that apply to each: **(many of the above)**

1. Spatial arrangement occurs when the writer describes a scene from his vantage and wishes the reader to see the same scene. To direct the reader, the author would use transitional expressions like *to my left, before me, on my right, above me,* and *above the mantle.* In Chapter Two of *Of Mice and Men,* John Steinbeck describes the bunkhouse that Candy shows Lenny and George:

The bunk house was a long, rectangular building. **Inside**, the walls were whitewashed and the floor unpainted. **In three walls** there were small, square windows, and in the fourth, a solid door with a wooden latch. **Against the walls** were eight bunks, five of them made up with blankets and the other three showing their burlap ticking. **Over** each bunk there was nailed an apple box with the opening forward so that it made two **shelves** for the personal belongings of the occupant of the bunk. And these shelves were loaded with little articles and talcum powder, razors and those Western magazines ranch men love to read and scoff at and secretly believe. And there were medicines on the **shelves**, and little vials, combs; and from nails on the box sides, a few neckties. Near one wall there was a black cast-iron stove, its top going straight up through the ceiling. **In the middle** of the room stood a big square table littered with playing cards, and around it were grouped boxes for the players to sit on.

2. Arrangement of details that range from most important to least important or vice-versa. An argument to convince, for example, might place the most important reason last as the "convincer"—the "zinger." Transitional expressions such as *most important, least important, first,* and *second* make the paragraph fluid and easy to follow.
3. Arrangement of details to create comparison, contrast, or comparison/contrast would include transitional expressions such as *on the contrary, on the other hand, likewise,* and *similarly.*

Rush Limbaugh and Bill Moyers differ as much as do minus and plus. Limbaugh's approach attacks, **but** Moyers defends the Constitution that gives journalists freedom of speech. Sometimes even, it seems that Mr. Limbaugh's choices of words come from the school ground rather than from the Halls of Ivy. For example, Linda Foley, the Newspaper Guild President, "that Linda Foley babe" in Limbaugh's parlance, felt a "rush" of slings and arrows because she had expressed concern for the journalists killed in Iraq. Moyers, with understandable standard English, consistently fights for the democratic principles by which this country succeeds and prospers. Limbaugh is, however, fun to hear because somewhere in his tirades he butchers the language and the meat taken home by the consumer is full of grizzle; Moyers is more than fun because his listeners leave with prime cuts, smooth, palatable, tender and good for the soul.

4. Arrangement of details by some kind of order, usually time, facilitates reading with transitional expressions such as *then, first (second, third), after,* and *before.*

The following four paragraphs, penned by Roxie Murphy Strackbein, one of my former students from the 1960s, is anecdotal and in time order with a whole bunch of facts and examples. The writing is exciting and, as I used to say, "All Roxie."

Looking back, I realize I should have seen it as a sign of things to come, an unveiling of my daughter's emerging personality. Innocently, I believed it was just a cute little story to share with family and friends. (I attribute this temporary lack of judgment to the fact that mothers frequently exist in a zombie-like state of bewilderment induced by inhaling toxic diaper fumes and having to retrieve "Flush Me" Elmo from the toilet on a regular basis.)

My daughter Jaime, who had just turned three, was busying herself in my closet as I hurried to leave for work and take her to daycare. She had a resourceful imagination and one of her favorite scenarios was to play with her doll, Heather. **While** she was thus engaged, she would become Debbie, Heather's mom. She was dressed up in my high heels to make her role as adult and mother all the more convincing. I attempted to get Jaime to put everything away so that we could leave, but she just left the shoes strewn on the bedroom floor. **When** I asked her to pick them up and put them back into the closet, she informed me that it was actually Heather who had been playing with the shoes. Feeling quite clever, if not a bit manipulative and guilty for taking advantage of a three-year-old, I explained that as Debbie, Heather's mom, she was responsible for what Heather did and that therefore she should put the shoes away. She coolly looked at me and replied, "I'm done playing Debbie and Heather, and since you are *my* mom, *you* are responsible to put the shoes away." Taken aback by her instant ability to apply such logic, I just chuckled, put the shoes away, and took her to day care.

Had I not been in such a hurry, would I have gained a critical insight about my daughter's "perfect storm" personality? Would I have realized that, for the remainder of her childhood and adolescent years, I would be held hostage by that unique blend of logic, stubbornness, and creativity? Could I have foreseen the times I would be called to the principal's office because she had focused her argumentative skills on the school bus driver in defense of a less outspoken fellow rider, or on the playground bully so that he would stop tormenting her friend? Would I have spent countless hours futilely attempting to enforce rules and curfews, only to have major doubts about my parenting skills after listening to her logically constructed and clearly presented arguments as to why things should be different?

Fortunately, time passes and my challenging three-year-old is now twenty-eight with children of her own. Her quests for truth, justice, and "The World According to Jaime" continue—more powerfully and effectively than ever. She has convinced more than fifty of her friends and family to boycott a local department store because she objected to their return policy, and she tackled the local and state school boards to have her children's school bus stop moved to a safer location. She confronted, cajoled, and conducted a battle strategy worthy of a West Point graduate, and after two refusals and a letter to her State Senator, she accomplished her mission. **During her most recent experience**, she researched and successfully executed the process of convincing an American-owned automobile manufacturing company to buy back her leaky SUV, which their local service agent had continually failed to repair. **After** hearing Jaime's presentation to the Arbitration Board, the company representative did not even attempt to present its case; she just apologized and wrote Jaime a check. At least **now** I am on the less turbulent side of Hurricane Jaime, where the winds are calmer and the seas less tumultuous. Believe it or not, I wholeheartedly admire her tenacity, strength, and desire to fight for what she believes; sometimes, however, I do wish she did not have to practice on me first!

Roxie lives in California and is a graphic designer par excellence. Her father Murph keeps me up to date on all the Murphy siblings and once every so often we all get together for a songfest at Lynch's. Roxie in high school was a cheerleader, an excellent student, a leader, and now one of my very good friends.

Had enough examples? Get writing. Write on "fog" as my former English teacher Chuck Collins once wrote the word on the board. Nothing else. No other directions. Just Write On! fog. The next day another word would appear.

So write. Write on anything—everything—wherever you are—every day—on the plane, boat, bus, train—but write.

This was a Poet — It is That
Distills amazing sense
From ordinary Meanings
                    Emily Dickinson

Chapter Five

LARGER UNITS (ESSAYS ET AL.)

Teacher: Write an editorial that encourages
school systems to lengthen the school day.

Using paragraphs to build pieces of literature has helped good writers succeed and poor writers fail. *The Catcher in the Rye* by J. D. Salinger starts with Holden Caufield talking with his psychiatrist and, at the same time to the reader, "Well, If you really want to hear about it. . . ." From that speech, Salinger developed a novel that has entertained and sometimes instructed students of all ages. Although supposedly narrated by a troubled teenager, the author's persona takes over immediately and constructs passages that remain memorable.

An essay writer like Ralph Waldo Emerson uses paragraphs in a more formal manner—he was a minister who wrote sermons at one time, then, as he put it, to be a better minister "I must leave the ministry"—his essay "On Self-Reliance" an example of his independence. One thing is clear, there is no set formula for stringing paragraphs together, but there are some generalizations that might help the beginning writer—and the pro—to write the Great American (or any other language) Novel or essay or biography or autobiography: Know your audience, keep the tone (attitude) consistent, write with a plan and an organization, and never write without observing human nature carefully.

Like sentences within the paragraphs, paragraphs must connect with each other; in other words, the writer must make transitions clear to the reader so that there are no misunderstandings. Mark Twain shows us in Chapter V of *Huckleberry Finn* where Huck meets his father after a long separation. Notice the transition accomplished with **pronouns**.

> I had shut the door to. Then I turned around, and there he was. I used to be scared of him all the time, he tanned me so much. I reckoned I was scared now, too; but in a minute I see I was mistaken. That is, after the first jolt, as you may say, when

my breath sort of hitched—**he** being so unexpected; but right away after, I see I warn't scared of him worth bothering about.

He was most fifty, and he looked it. His hair was long and tangled and greasy, and hung down, and you could see his eyes shining through like he was behind vines. It was all black, no gray, so was his long, mixed-up whiskers. There warn't no color in his face, where **his** face showed; it was white; not like another man's white, but a white to make a body sick, a white to make a body's flesh crawl—a tree-toad white, a fish-belly white. As for his clothes—just rags, that was all. **He** had one ankle resting on 'tother knee; the boot on that foot was busted, and two of his toes stuck through, and he worked them now and then. His hat was laying on the floor; an old black slouch with the top caved in, like a lid.

I stood a-looking at **him**; **he** set there a-looking at me, with **his** chair tilted back a little. I set the candle down. I noticed the window was up; so **he** had clumb in by the shed.

THE NEW SAT WRITING SECTION

The new SAT Writing test format we used at Hand High School in the 1970s, 1980s, and 1990s to determine sophomore competency in writing. Given a prompt, words of a great poet, essayist, novelist, speaker, et al., the student had twenty-five minutes to **justify,** that is, to prove the truth of the statement. In the new SAT, the student is given two points of view and must defend one or the other.

> Success is counted sweetest
> By those who ne'er succeed.

The above quotation from Emily Dickinson proved tough for a few because the first task of the sophomores was to try to grasp the sense of the words. Some misinterpreted, some just did not know what the author meant, but the majority of students began writing almost immediately. The results were astounding, not because most of us in the English Department used this method on tests and in writing units, but because the students had performed this exercise since about the fifth grade.

Now students are given two sides of a prompt, pro or con. The task is to decide which side to argue.

Example Essay Prompt: Think carefully about the issue presented in the following words from Emily Dickinson. Then read the assignment.

> They say that "Time assuages"—
> Time never did assuage—
> An actual suffering strengthens
> As sinews do with age—
>
> Time is a Test of Trouble—
> But not a Remedy—
> If such it prove, it prove too
> There was no Malady—

Assignment: Does time ease the pain of a dire situation, or do the trials one goes through make the person stronger? Plan and write an essay in which you develop your point of view on this issue. Support your position with reasoning and examples taken from your reading, studies, experience, or observations.

Based on the given directions, students should not begin writing at once but should plan, with an informal outline, a strategy. Some juniors in American Lit—Honors participated with this prompt. Here is the best response:

". . . An actual suffering strengthens / As sinews do with age. . . ." These two lines from Emily Dickinson's poem present the argument that through suffering, one's character becomes stronger. Although some argue that with time pain from a misfortunate situation can fade (which is the other argument presented in Dickinson's poem), the sufferer tends to emerge from pain a stronger, more accepting person. Through literature and personal experience, I realize that suffering, however painful, eventually proves to be a tool for creating a stronger emotional source in the sufferer.

In *The Scarlet Letter* by Nathaniel Hawthorne, the main character, Hester Prynne, is plagued by the prison sentence that forces her to wear forever a scarlet letter "A" sewn to her clothing. This symbol of rejection that sets her apart from her community causes Hester much embarrassment. She comments on how, when she first receives her wretched punishment that strips her pride, the townspeople and travelers give her dirty looks and treat her disdainfully. As the story continues though, Hester begins to absorb the dirty glances and harsh treatment without noticing. In a sense, her suffering caused by the scarlet letter has caused her to become strong enough emotionally to ignore completely her situation. Hester's suffering made her stronger.

Similarly, in *The Lovely Bones*, a family must deal with the loss of a child. The Salmon's daughter disappears when, unknown to the family, she is raped and killed by a neighbor and buried. In the beginning of the story, the Salmon's seem unable to cope with their loss, and the family begins to fall apart. The mother moves out, the sister starts to get into trouble at school, and the father becomes a workaholic. As the story continues, the Salmons begin to cope with the pain, and, although it never ceases, the pain causes the family's characters to strengthen. By the end of the story, the family is still plagued with the pain, but they are able to cope because of their newfound emotional stability.

I have also discovered that suffering makes one stronger. Two years ago, my aunt, uncle, and cousins, with whom I was very close, were suddenly killed in a car accident. My family and I went through the typical mourning period, and to this day the pain hasn't lessened. But I have found that now, two years later, I am able to accept their deaths, although I still miss them terribly. I also feel as if, now that I have experienced this tragedy, I am emotionally stable enough to go through such pain again. As a result, when I found out that my grandmother had cancer, the situation was easier to handle because of the previous incident.

In conclusion, while pain may fade for some over time, I have found that the travail makes a person stronger through reading and personal experience.

Not bad for twenty minutes of writing under pressure! Becky Jablonski, at the time of the writing, was a junior at Daniel Hand High School. Her teacher was Ray Dudley, a thirty-plus-year veteran.

This paper should receive the highest score for several reasons. First, active verbs abound; passive verbs are used judiciously. Second, her examples show her to be an excellent student. Third, her use of punctuation is nearly perfect. The only errors that were corrected were the two split infinitives (a topic that might be argued—but please, with someone else), the spelling, "althought," and throwing a preposition away from its object (which I threw back). I also realize that the critics judge "holistically," giving an overall impression of the papers, but certainly egregious grammatical errors do play a part. There is no question in my mind that Becky will be a writer professionally.

WRITING OFFICE (WHATEVER THE "OFFICE" IS) MEMOS

Writing memos has long been an indirect means of communication. Writers of the memo, usually a boss or mentor of some kind, should keep in mind the audience they are addressing. Beginning with "ATTN" might seem military, while beginning with "Hey, dudes" might turn the stomachs of some. Knowing one's audience, then, is critical.

In the 1970s, a former principal sent a memo through the mail boxes in the front office. The secretaries placed the dittoed memo in the mailbox assigned to each teacher. During this time, the administration and staff were about to launch a brand-new scheduling process. The memo, received that Monday morning, read: "With the advent of the new schedule, we have a <u>magnanimous</u> job ahead of us." Not a very good memo from someone whose name began with "Dr." The English Department was magnanimous, however, when we did not make too much fun of him.

E-MAIL

Former students say that when they e-mail me, they feel pressure to write everything correctly. Then there are others who, for one reason or another, could not care less. E-mail might be the salvaging or the destruction of writing: For those who write to friends or relatives, without regard for spelling, grammar, syntax, and so on, transition to formal writing becomes almost impossible; for those who take the time during the e-mailing, they can use the experience to practice good writing.

Kim Blondin, one of my favorite students of all time because of the dramatic change she went through in her junior year from becoming a nonreader to a prolific reader in one quick assignment, recently wrote the following e-mail about a skydiving incident:

I decided to go skydiving with two of my best friends, one who had previously jumped and my friend & I it was our first. So, we arrive at North Hampton Mass in the morning, watched a 25 minute video on how dangerous this is. With that in mind I began to feel a rush of adrenalin & fear at the same time. Well the time came to do it. My friends went first & had a blast, the look on their faces was priceless they had just done something that you only talk about doing. It was my turn, I got in this plane, which was not very big attached to a man I had known for 4 hours. We left the ground & that was where it was no turning back. At 9000 feet they put the plane in idle and opened the shade—the door was a shade! I took one look out & that was it. I screamed a scream that came from my toes, a scream of complete fear & excitement. 10 seconds later my arms were being pulled out & I opened my eyes to see that things were so small below & I was flying in the sky. I then realized that I had accomplished something that changed my life in the fact that life is only how you choose to live it & by taking chances. Even ones that are scary you never know until you take them. As my father would say "the sky is the limit"

I think she had a great time.

GRANT WRITING

Do you need money for a project? Write a grant proposal. Simple? Yes and no.

The first consideration is need: For what is the money needed? Second, once having identified the need, you should explore the various funding agencies to determine what kind of programs they have donated to; in other words, what is the mission statement of each agency under consideration? To be more specific, let's take a look at the mission statement of The Schumann Foundation, from Bob Schumann himself:

> The Schumann Foundation donates funds to foster media that demand truth from our political system.

If you plan to write a grant, then, there are certain criteria, and the first is do not go after monies for your personal gain. The people who respond to your media are the benefactors—not you. Once that rule is determined, the foundation should know exactly what the purpose for the money is. You know, but do they?

Once outlined and written, the project might be worthless if it does not look right, if there are glaring language errors, or if it is just not presentable and logical. It might not be a bad idea to have an English professor help you with the wording. Double space it, make it look nice, and hope for the best. Your letter of introduction might be as important as the project itself.

Finally, and perhaps above all, try to determine the tone, the attitude of the grantor. If your presentation is diametrically opposed in philosophy, it will not stand a chance. Good luck.

SCIENTIFIC WRITING

Scientific writing demands expert knowledge. If you write a report of a study—let's say on mussels—you'd better know what has been studied before and how your study adds to already gained knowledge. Who better to help me with this (he already has in Chapter Four) than Dr. Tom Suchanek, a graduate of Durham (Connecticut) High School, Class of '65 (and a degree holder from University of Connecticut—B.S. in biology, SUNY—M.S. in ecology and evolution, and University of Washington—Ph.D. in zoology). Notice that in scientific writing, since the emphasis is on that which is studied (and not the person who studies it), the passive voice is used almost exclusively.

I could not possibly have written the following, but I do eat mussels by the bushel:

> In many space-limited marine systems, plants and animals are often used as a substratum by other organisms (epiphytes and epizoans). Mussels are frequently overgrown by epizoans because they are sessile and present a large area of hard substratum for attachment (Suchanek, 1979). The effect of the epizoan on the underlying host organism may be positive, neutral, or negative. A common benefit of epizoism is protection from predation (Ross, 1971; Bloom, 1975; Vance, 1978). Frequently tubiculosis polychaetes, bryozoans, and other

colonial invertebrate epizoans do not have any appreciable effect on their hosts (Seed and O'Connor, 1981).

AUTOBIOGRAPHY (BIOGRAPHY)

Possibly the only differences between these two genres are person and, therefore, perspective. One of my dear friends, Kippy Martin (*Superwoman Does Not Exist*), grew up in the Bronx, but is more than just a Yankee fan and wrote the following:

> The Bronx—it started as a nightmare and ended preparing me for the real world. In the beginning we unloaded boxes and furniture into a three-bedroom, five-floor walkup. Our front yard had changed from a grassy green lawn to a community with buildings, parked cars, and concrete sidewalks. Our ears heard no more the squeaky crickets and the comforting sounds from sundown to sunup; now the Jerome Avenue Subway, loud street discussions of no consequence, and more than an occasional siren made the night eerie. I awoke every morning to critters who felt they owned the apartment and seemed to wish *we* would move.
>
> It was a diverse community that accepted me, regardless of the color of my skin or the texture of my hair. Those ten years in the Bronx provided me with survival skills I would use the rest of my life. By the age of thirteen, I was cooking, traveling on trains and busses, babysitting for younger siblings, and avoiding dangerous situations. The Bronx, although very different, taught me to adapt to new environments, to use patience and humor to extricate me out of any situation, and most of all to be thankful.
>
> Then I moved to Madison, Connecticut . . .

Cover Letters for Job Applications

The other day I was surfing "cover letters" and was astounded and appalled that there were cover letters all set for the job applicants. All they had to do was download the letter, change a few words to personalize the letter, and doctor it up enough so that it looked official.

Then I started to think: Suppose I was applying for a job, lifted the letter from the web site, covered my resume with it, and handed it to a future employer. Then, what would have happened if several others showed up with the same letter? The future boss would just shake a head and send us all walking.

Besides, the taking of others' writings as if they were your own is plagiarism.

Advice: Write your own cover letter and then, if you're not sure of yourself and your writing, take it to your former English teacher and ask for help.

Letters to the Editor

Every year, some friends will call for help in writing a letter to an editor. Most do not really need help, but the issue, pressing at the time, needs words for or against or praise or denigration, and the writers want advice.

Usually, there are very few errors. The errata that do occur show up as typos, an occasional agreement problem with indefinite pronouns, or the use of the passive voice when the active voice would be more effective.

Here is an example lent to me by a very good friend, Bob Maloney. He lauds a future candidate for the Board of Finance:

A reassuring facet of our town government is the checks-and-balances the Board of Finance has over the first select-man's [*Editor's note*: Tom Scarpati is the present first selectman] budget requests. Sadly, this taxpayer's line of defense is being compromised. Pray tell, how can Board of Finance Jennifer Tung [Tom Scarpati's campaign manager] and Fillmore McPherson [Scarpati's treasurer] be expected to impartially vote on the first selectman's spending propos-als? Should Madison risk having political foxes guarding the budget hen house? I don't think so!

That's why many voters, including Republican Town Committee members like myself, support Emile Geisen-heimer's candidacy. . . . Emile will hit the ground running. He has valuable past experience with Madison's budgeting process as a police commissioner. There will be no learning curve for Emile. He'll make an immediate impact, an impact that is free from political obligations.

If Madisonites want proven expertise, ethical objectiv-ity, and a public office holder experience representing them on the Board of Finance, Emile Geiseheimer's the one.

The split infinitive notwithstanding, Bob's point is clear, forceful, and obviously one-sided, which, he said, "I intended."

Writing, then, takes various forms and demands, for the most, precision so that the writer conveys exact thoughts to whoever the reader is. What will be your next assignment?

HOW TO WRITE A NEWS ARTICLE

The proper structure of a news article, as any first-semester journalism student knows, is the inverted pyramid: the most salient facts on top, narrowing to important but non-essential information and closing with finer details. This presentation allows the reader to glean what he needs to know in the first few paragraphs and decide whether to read on or move to the next story. Thus a first sentence might read: DOGPATCH, June 11—The fugitive wanted for the murder of eleven people in seven states was captured in an abandoned factory here, local police announced today. Increasingly, however, reporters write more like aspiring novelists that journalists, so the the first sentence of the same story might read: DOGPATCH, June 11—The summer sun fades gently through the dusty haze of this Midwestern hamlet, where the prospect of murder is as distant as the shouts of Little Leaguers practicing on the field by the shuttered flywheel factory, an unsightly reminder of the town's faded industrial glory. A degree of descriptive flair has long been accepted in Sunday editions when the leisurely pace of the day presumably renders the reader amenable to a more circuitous path to the news. But the practice has rambled out of control and now seems the rule rather than the exception. Exactly why publishers and editors think their customers wish to indulge reporters' dubious literary pretensions remains a mystery. Nevertheless, correspondents routinely subject their readers to tedious scene-setting before meandering into the meat of the matter and trailing off once again in trifle. The inverted pyramid has morphed into an inverted hourglass, a shape as appealing to serious readers of the news as it would be to a judge of the swimsuit competition.

(Steve Allis. Reprinted with permission.)

There is a word
Which bears a sword
Can pierce an armed man—
                    Emily Dickinson

Chapter Six

PUNCTUATION AND MECHANICS: ALL YOU REALLY NEED TO KNOW

Teacher to student: A colon is a punctuation mark!
Wise student to teacher: I thought it was a plantation
owner—at least that's what Webster's says.

Number 278
A word is dead, when it is said
Some say—
I say it just begins to live
That day

Emily Dickinson, circa 1872

If any title be appropriate for this astonishing poem, I might suggest "Birth." Emily Dickinson's metaphor of language and the birthing process emerges because of the punctuation in the poem, not typical of her because most of her poems she sprinkled with dashes going every which way.

The first stanza contains a comma and a dash, halting the flow of her words. These interruptions, like contractions mothers experience, begin and end although perhaps not as abruptly as in Dickinson's shortest piece. The punctuation, however, speaks to us powerfully; the "breaks" are precisely chosen and convey exactly what the writer intended, and unlike the majority of her work that was not published during her lifetime, this poem might have been destined for publication rather than being included in a neat little bundle found in the attic after her death.

The second stanza has no punctuation. The birth of the word has come alive "that day." The flow of the words is not interrupted. The absence of the punctuation seems as important in this stanza as the punctuation in the first stanza.

Have I gone too far with interpretation? Perhaps, but one must remember that Emily Dickinson reigns as the queen of American poetry. She loved words, even coined a few ("a convenient grass"— the only time the noun "grass" was ever preceded by "a"), and often, when hearing or reading a particularly choice word, said, "There's a word to which you can take your hat off." Moreover, she knew the rules of punctuation, as almost all writers do, and made up her own style of mechanics ("It's unobtrusive Mass"; "did'nt").

This short sentence helps prove the importance, nay the necessity, of punctuation:

A woman without her man is nothing.

In fact, during a unit on punctuation, I would write that sentence on the board among shouts from the girls in the class and guffaws from the boys. After the hubbub subsided, I would ask, "Can punctuation change the meaning of words?" The initial answers usually were negative until some students began shifting the words around and then using some internal punctuation, and sometime during the class a student would arrive at the following:

A woman—without her, man is nothing.

And the shouts turned to finger pointing and the guffaws shifted.

Therefore, unlike some authors who dislike certain punctuation marks and do not use them, this author and this book embrace all punctuation marks, and, borrowing from the "Redheaded Belle of Amherst," say, "Here are some punctuation marks to which you can tip your hat."

THE COMMA (,)

We might as well start with the comma because more controversy arises from this little mark than from major White House decisions, and what better source than the *Oxford English Dictionary*:

> The function of the comma is to make clear the grammatical structure, and hence the sense, of the passage; one of the means by which this is effected in actual speech is a short

pause; hence the comma is often inaccurately said to be merely the mark of such a pause.

Words, Phrases, Clauses, and Sentences in a Series

What better place, then, to start with the comma than grammatical items in a series (three or more): words, phrases, clauses, and sentences.

Words

Note: In items in a series, so that there is no question or problem, a comma will be placed always before the coordinating conjunction.

> Judy Semler volunteered to bring food, blankets, one grill, a game of quoits, a first aid kit, and hot chocolate to the annual Guilford Charities picnic. (nouns)

> Brash, confident, physically fit, and ready for action, Mark Mulvey warmed up for the Geneva Marathon. (adjectives)

> Anne Mulvey baked cookies, cleaned the pool, washed the car, shopped at Migros, and napped for three hours all in one day. (verbs)

Phrases

> On top of the mountain, in the trees, off the water, and against the clouds, the sun painted a series of pictures worthy of Monet. (prepositional phrases—notice the last one has a comma after it because the series begins the sentence)

> Breathing rapidly, stretching diligently, dressing lightly, and eating nothing prepared Erin Mulvey for her walk benefiting MADD. (gerund phrases—note that after the last one there is no comma because subjects are not separated from the verbs)

Writing lengthy novels, carving furniture with his teeth, and living in the heart of Paris, Victor Hugo became a folk hero of sorts. (participial phrases)

To write a novel, to play Major League baseball, and to live comfortably gave focus to my life. (infinitive phrases)

Clauses

Ronald Edward Catania, who catches more fish than anyone else, who cuts hair better than any other hairdresser, and who collects more toys than any child could, loves Mario's Place in Westport, Connecticut. (adjective clauses)

After he showered for about an hour, after he moaned through a half-hour massage, and after he had rested for fifteen minutes, Peter Newcomb readied himself for packing down a Bud or two. (adverb clauses)

Whoever caused the turmoil at the police department, whoever burned the hole in the wall, and whoever stole the computer from the department store were asked to come forward and admit their guilt. (noun clauses)

Sentences

When joined, two or more simple sentences become compound sentences, and then when subordinate clauses are added, they can become compound/complex sentences. (More about that topic is covered in Chapter Three.) Concentration here will join two or more sentences, first using coordination conjunctions (*but, and, or, nor, for, yet*); notice that when sentences are joined with these **conjunctions**, the writer must use a comma.

Bobby Bushnell caught forty-five stripers in one fishing trip, **but** his mate lost all of his fish.

Sue Quatrano took her mother in the Zodiak, **and** her mother responded by taking Sue for a ride in the new car.

Doug Walker made several repairs to the dock at his own expense, **or** he was going to move to another marina.

Richie Hahn refused the bottle of Jack Daniels, **nor** would he take any money for extricating the nest of bees near the community hose.

Barbara Walker installed her own nail polishing service at the dock, **for** there were enough customers to take advantage of the service.

Tony Barone hops from boat to boat like a monkey, **yet** his knees were in terrible shape.

Introductory Adverb Phrases and Clauses Set Off by Commas

Generally, a comma is used to separate an introductory adverb phrase or clause from the rest of the sentence. Short introductory adverb phrases sometimes really do not need commas unless without the commas there would be confusion or even comedy.

> **Adverb phrase:** Because of her commitment to teaching gymnastics, Judy Sembler often takes her family to dinner.

After studying great writers for three weeks, Harold Battenfield wrote the Great American Novel.

To confuse the obese, gray-haired bartender at Lynch's, Richard A. Richo tipped him with Susan B. Anthony dollars.

Short Adverb phrase: After hours the band signed autographs. (Comma is not needed because there is no confusion.)

Before starting, the driver should choke the engine. (Notice here that a comma is absolutely necessary.)

Adverb clause: Although the crossword puzzle baffled most of her neighbors, Mary Battenfield finished it in three minutes.

Whenever William Evert Sunblade spoke about the Red Sox, he was roundly booed by the breakfast patrons at Circle Pizza.

Because Laura Antionette Sunblade exuded confidence with the IBM copier, she was voted "Copyist of the Year" ten years in a row.

When the adverb clause comes at the end of the sentence, a comma is used if the clause is in opposition to the clause before it. Otherwise, a comma is not needed:

Joe Frank Bruno has been elected to the Bartender's Hall of Fame, even though he does not qualify.

Matt DeCapua aspires to act on Broadway because he knows fame will follow.

The Comma with Adjective Phrases and Clauses

Now, "restrictive" and "nonrestrictive," semitechnical terms, come to the fore. I never knew what they meant until Chuck Collins, my senior English teacher, explained them away: "If the phrase or clause can be dropped from the sentence without changing the meaning of the noun it modifies, the phrase or clause should have commas. If you drop the phrase or the clause and the meaning is clearly altered, do not use commas. The first is nonrestrictive and the latter is restrictive," he would expound.

> **Restrictive phrase:** The man <u>sitting next to Jose B. Cosio on the plane from Helsinki</u> did not know what to make of him. (No commas are needed because the meaning would be completely changed—the question would immediately arise, "What man?")

> **Restrictive clause:** Mark Yallum, <u>who works for the New York State Liquor Authority</u>, once owned night clubs in Paris. (Commas are needed because the underlined clause could be dropped from the sentence without changing the meaning.)

Note: Good writers know the difference between restrictive and nonrestrictive ("essential" and "nonessential" seem better labels) phrases and clauses. With clauses, the word *that* should always introduce an essential clause, while *which* should always introduce a nonessential clause.

> **Nonessential clause:** Linda Eleonor Barlind, tour director extraordinaire, directed our tour of Denmark to the statue of the "Little Mermaid," <u>which once was beheaded by an unknown hooligan</u>. (Interesting tidbit about the statue—but not necessary to the meaning of the sentence.)

> **Essential clause:** The market <u>that opens every day near the Harbor of Bergen, Norway</u>, is the oldest outdoor market in the world. (You would never know where the market was—in fact, it could be any market, anywhere.)

Commas and Quotation Marks (" ")

In 99 percent of writing, the comma (and the period) will be placed inside the quotation marks. In the four examples that follow, words are directly quoted from actual conversations with the persons involved. Note the position of the commas, especially those introducing the speech:

> "Comedy is the spice of life," said Frank DeCapua one day.
>
> Sean E. Donlan proclaimed, "Law is everything."
>
> "Sean steps on my feet when we dance," complained Maggie Seekamp. "I still love his moves, though."
>
> "I really like Dan," offered Omar W. Francis, "but I wish he'd brush his teeth on occasions."

Those are the basics with commas and quoted speeches. It really does not matter if the speeches are voiced or internal either:

> Donna Francis thought, "What if nothing happened?"
>
> "We do not know that," mused Arthur B. Haesche.

Commas in Compound Sentences

In compound sentences, commas are mostly needed to separate two or more main clauses—but if the clauses are short and closely related, a comma is not needed. Many novelists eschew the comma in these situations and use them only when there might be some confusion.

> Russell Cox prefers Chardonnay but Roxanne Servidio-Cox likes Pinot. (Since the clauses are short and close in meaning, no comma is needed. You could put one there if you wanted, however.)

Ron Catalano thinks Afros are cool, but Ronald Edward Catania thinks they're out of date.

The Lappi Ravintola in Helsinki serves the best reindeer steaks imaginable, and its other specialties include seal steak and elk pate, and its desserts are second to none.

In 2004, Ron Artest flew into the stands in Detroit and pummeled some innocent fans, and the referees were helpless to stop the fracas. (Even a newspaper, which tends to avoid commas, must have one here; otherwise, the referees seem as if they're being pummeled.)

But look at the following:

In 2004, Ron Artest flew into the stands in Detroit and the referees were helpless to stop the fracas. (Here it is clear what is happening, and the comma could be left out.)

If there are a number of main clauses (more than two), then commas must separate each clause from the other:

Richard Gibbons works in and around London, Gloria Gibbons lights up a room with her entrance, Rachel Gibbons was the best student in her class in high school, and Gee Collins has a reputation of performing greatness on the playing fields.

Commas and Introductory Participial Phrases

Introductory participial phrases should be set off by commas. The only exception occurs when the introductory phrase comes immediately before the verb. It then looks like a gerund phrase, but is not.

<u>Bringing up the rear to ensure everyone was on the bus</u>, Claes Douglas Barlind sacrificed himself for the good of others.

> Traveling in the United States almost every two years, Rita and Ib Mejding of Copenhagen could give lectures on the canyons of the West.

> *but*

> Bringing up the rear were Andy and Diane Melrose because Andy was always looking for a newspaper.

Commas and Parenthetical Expressions

Parenthetical expressions, called **asides** in theater, interrupt the flow of the sentence and usually are spoken rather that written. That is not to say they cannot be written.

> Martin Leach, to say the least, enjoys traveling more than the average person.

> Whenever Richard Cory went downtown, so far as I know, we people on the pavement looked at him.

> John and Janice Carletti, I believe, are two of the funniest people I have ever met.

We must include here some introductory expressions that are set off by commas, such as *well, however,* and *oh.*

> Well, if you insist, I might.

> Oh, what a beautiful morning!

But with just plain "O," no comma is needed:

> O ancient warrior!

Some of the other interrupters:

> Parsnips, on the other hand, sometimes are tasteless.

Bob Wigham, <u>indeed</u>, builds better boats than does Rampage.

The Red Sox, <u>after all</u>, should have won something.

Direct Address (Apostrophe) and Commas

Direct address means that someone is talked to in some tone. **Apostrophe** is the term used to indicate someone talked to, whether that person or group is really there or not.

> <u>Ladies and gentlemen of the jury</u>, have you reached a verdict?
>
> <u>Gentlemen</u>, lend me your ears.
>
> <u>Lord</u>, please help me!
>
> Let me warn you, <u>students</u>, that fooling the teacher is wrong.
>
> I warned you, <u>my fine-feathered enemy</u>!

Adjectives and Adverbs with Commas

Sentences beginning with <u>adverbs or adjectives</u> usually see these set off by commas:

> **Adjectives:** <u>Ebullient</u> and <u>friendly</u>, Connie Rogers lights up a room when she enters.
>
> <u>Talented</u> and <u>resourceful</u>, Al Rogers once treated several hundred of his friends to a sax concert. (I had to be very careful with that example.)
>
> **Adverbs:** <u>Meticulously</u> and <u>with perseverance</u>, Chris Beebe creates gardens that should be in magazines.
>
> <u>Proudly</u> and <u>sincerely</u>, Jack Beebe relates to anyone who listens to stories about antique cars.

With adjectives in a series, sometimes it is up to the writer to use or not to use commas. For example:

Laurent George O'Shea decided that he would pave his driveway to look like a long, yellow brick road. (The comma here could be avoided because one might consider "yellow brick road" close to a compound noun and therefore "long," the lone adjective, need not be set off—decisions, decisions.)

But in the following example, a few commas are needed:

Elizabeth O'Shea, working in her gardens, once spotted a huge, one-legged, tailless, wide-eyed fawn.

Miscellaneous Uses of the Comma

- Commas set off items in an address: Dan and Nancy Mulvey have lived at 123 Smith Street, Anywhere, Connecticut, for over forty years. On an envelope, of course, these items would be in list form and only one comma would be needed. Also, there is no comma needed between the state and the zip code.

- Commas set off items in dates: On January 10, 1942, nothing happened.

- Commas set off persons from their occupations: Debra Dion, a jockey, Nicole Bongiovanni, a flower designer, and Kina Gevaert, an athlete, hang out together.

- When words are left out, sometimes a comma takes over: Matt DeCapua has starred in many dramatic roles, his father none.

- The following expressions are set off by commas from the rest of the sentence: *e.g.*, *that is*, *namely* (a priest at Providence College we called Father Namely used this expression willy-nilly in his sermons and in his lectures), and *i.e.* By the way, *e.g.* is from the Latin meaning "exempli gratis"—for example; *i.e.*, also from the Latin, means "id est,"—that is.

  > Lenny Wilkens has played for and coached many teams, <u>namely</u>, Providence College, St. Louis Hawks, Seattle Super-Sonics, Portland Trail Blazers, Cleveland Cavaliers, Atlanta Hawks, Toronto Raptors, and the New York Knicks.
  >
  > Bobby Nilson lived in Saigon with Mark Mulvey—<u>that is</u>, they lived and played together.
  >
  > Jonathan Mulvey attends school in Florida—<u>i.e.</u>, he attends a school that is in the vicinity of ten golf courses.
  >
  > Ann Mulvey speaks all sorts of languages—<u>e.g.</u>, French, English, Spanish, Swahili, and a cross between Arabic and Gypsy.

- Contrasting expressions are set off by commas: Baseball, not basketball or football, is America's game.

- At the beginning and end of personal letters, commas are used:

  > Dear Aunt Dorothy,
  > Sincerely yours,

THE COLON (:)

1. In formal letters, the salutation (the greeting) is followed by a colon:

   Dear Sir:
   To the Townspeople of Madison:
   Dear Parents:

2. A large number of words quoted are introduced by a colon:

   Rene Descartes once wrote: "The reason joy causes us to flush (is that) Joy thus makes the colour more vivid and more ruddy, because in opening the sluices of the heart it causes the blood to flow more quickly in all the veins, and because, becoming warmer and more subtle, it moderately distends all the parts of the face, and thus gives it a more cheerful and lively expression."

3. Biblical passages, the chapter and verse, are separated by a colon:

   Matthew 12:26 (Chapter 12 of Matthew, verse 26)
   Rev. 3:7–13 (Chapter 3 of Revelations, verses 7 to 13)

4. When a character in a play or movie script speaks, a colon separates that character from his speech:

   Lady Macduff: Sirrah, your father's dead;
                   And what will you do now? How will
                   you live?
   Son: As birds do, Mother.

Lady Macduff:	What, with worms and flies?
Son:	With what I get, I mean; and so do they.

5. In word analogies, one colon is translated as "is to," and two consecutive colons means "as."

    grandfather : alligator :: grandmother : crocodile
    baseball : national pastime :: hockey : prizefighting

6. Two separate main clauses can be separated by a colon if the second clause explains, amplifies, or illustrates an idea in the first clause.

    Gerald Joseph "Gee" Collins epitomizes the perfect handyman: His roof waterproofing at the Dolly Madison lasted fourteen hours.

    In 2005, the New York Mets equaled the money output of the Yankees: The acquisition of Carlos Beltran and Pedro Martinez rivaled the Yankees' acquisition of Randy Johnson and Tino Martinez.

7. Items in a series are introduced by a colon.

    Judith Ann Collins reigns supreme when in a social situation: She exudes confidence in conversation, never uses sweeping generalizations, and endears herself to every listener.

8. When a form of "follow" (*as follows, the following*) ends a statement, a colon follows:

    Kathleen Boyhan-Maus relaxes in situations like the following: extreme horror movies, twenty-mile backed-up traffic, and can openers that do not work.

The Period (.)

A period indicates a complete stop. Period. End of sentence. New sentence following.

> Stephan Eric "Roadkill" Lindberg thinks the best vacation is a seven-week stay in New York City.
>
> Constance McCree Mermann Vitale, on the other hand, relishes the relative quiet of Vermont. (These are called **declarative** sentences because they declare or state something positive or negative.)

Besides ending declarative sentences, a period is used to end both an indirect question or statement and a command or imperative sentence.

> **Indirect statement:** Joanne Tolles Fox used to say that teaching at Coginchaug Regional High School was a challenge and a half. (Those were not precisely the words Joanne used, but they were close.)
>
> **Indirect question:** Margaret Tolles Greim Hannigan asked if the pleasantly plump bartender was behind the stick at Lynch's. (Again, these probably were not her exact words, but they were close.)
>
> **Command or imperative sentence:** Leave your book on the desk and follow me. (Someone or some animal is urged to do something.)

A period is used after numbers or letters in a list (especially in an outline).

    I. Discover
   II. Analyze
       A. Behave
       B. Look happy

Inside parentheses within another sentence, a period is not needed, even though what is inside the parentheses is a sentence:

> Jeff Leonard Greim (he would not admit it) loves to play the horses.

> Courtney Victoria Collins pitched eight no hitters (she claims nineteen) in high school.

QUESTION MARK (?)

When someone asks a question or doubts something, a question mark is used.

> Ambrose Bierce (1842–1914?) (The question mark means that no one is sure when Mr. Bierce died.)

> When did Ambrose Bierce die? (a direct question)

The positioning of the question mark when it is used with quotation marks depends on the nature of the quote.

> Jeralyn Frances Krygier asked, "What is for lunch?" (The question mark is inside the quotation marks because the direct question was quoted.)

> Why did Alyssa Artiano laugh when she said, "I take marriage very seriously"? (The question mark is outside the quote because the quoted part is not a question—but the entire sentence is.)

You're funny? You're funny! (The first question throws doubt to whoever "you" is; the second statement throws no doubt.)

EXCLAMATION POINT (!)

This punctuation mark shows some form of emotion and turns a sentence or a question into a bit of hype.

> Robert and Brenda Collins love eating breakfast at the Dolly. (Maybe they don't like it that much.)
>
> Robert and Brenda Collins love eating breakfast at the Dolly! (They really like it here.)

The exclamation point turns an ordinary question into a question asked somewhat excitedly:

> Why did you forget your homework? (Ho hum)
>
> Why did you forget your homework! (In other words, what is wrong with you!)

THE DASH (—)

The dash should be used sparingly, perhaps more in an e-mail than in a formal paper. Usually to indicate a sudden break in thought, the dash (and the hyphen) has specific uses.

1. To show not only a sudden break in thought but a change in syntax:

> Deborah Ramsay McGuire—how beautiful a name to sing!
>
> George R. Brown Jr.—he has fought to restore Providence College baseball—continues to pursue his dream.

During the nineties—perhaps at the beginning of the decade—Jan Anne Keane rowed her kayak several hundred nautical miles.

2. To indicate an interruption in speech:

Beverly Ann Mahan Bakes said, "I believe it is my turn to purchase a—"

"Purchase a what?" interrupted Gerald Arthur Bakes.

3. To emphasize a particular element by repeating the element after the dash:

Julia Jane Bakes volunteered to chair the convention—the convention to celebrate great writing at Central Connecticut State College.

Diane Lois Doyle devised a real estate plan that was innovative and simple—innovative because no one had dreamed it would work and simple because it had been done before.

4. To indicate that the collective pronouns summarize the nouns that precede the dash:

Lawrence Craig Parker Jr., Christina Mary Florence Isadora Parker, Graham Horton—*all* were familiar with the Pine Orchard area.

The words the happy say
Are paltry melody
But those the silent feel
Are beautiful—

Emily Dickinson

Chapter Seven

COMMON MISTAKES TO AVOID!
THE BIG THREE (AND THEN SOME)

Son: Mom, I'm going to lay down.
Mom (to herself): A foundation?

NUMBER ONE: GENERAL REFERENCE OF PRONOUNS (THE MISUSE OF WHICH, THAT, AND IT)

Books about language and grammar fascinate me. *Eats Shoots & Leaves* was no exception, and the fascination increased when I saw some language errors:

> Meanwhile, the full stop [the period] is surely the simplest mark to understand—so long as everyone continues to have some idea what a sentence is, which is a condition that can't be guaranteed.
>
> from *Eats Shoots & Leaves* by Lynne Truss

As a grammarian of sorts, I took exception to the use of the word "which," which is used incorrectly. First, the reader has no clue to what "which" is referring. Is it "idea"? "Sentence"? "The full stop [the period] is surely the simplest mark"? However, none of these words fit the referral. Going back over the text then, the reader perhaps now sees the meaning. The author of this quote is referring to the idea, the generalization if you will, that most readers know what a sentence is.

For thirty-seven years, I taught that general referencing of pronouns, like the example above, was an egregious error, softened only by the fact that thousands of writers included this kind of mistake in their writings, and then listening to a student say, "If Matthew Arnold does it, why can't I?" To that student I would say, "Would you jump from a mountain because someone else did? The word *which* (or *that* or *it*) must refer to a specific word and not a general idea; *which* or *that* can refer to plurals, but *it* always refers to a singular word."

Even Bill Moyers, in his latest *Moyers on America*, generalizes *that*.

> That era of a wide-open and crowded newspaper playing field began to fade as the old hand presses gave way to giant machines with press runs and readerships in the hundreds of thousands and costs in the millions. But <u>that</u> doesn't necessarily or immediately kill public-spirited journalism. . . . [underscore is mine]

The word "that," singular or plural, should refer only to a singular or plural noun. I see "era" and "field," but "presses" and "machines" or even "press runs" might be candidates for "that." A simple addition of "fact" after "that" clears the air.

Even in the made-up world of grammar books, an example can be relevant:

> My father lusted after every female in the neighborhood, my mother sainted her existence through her children, and my aunts and uncles defended both of them. It made me wonder about values.

"It" has no reference. "It" is third-person singular. "Father," "female," and "neighborhood," are third-person singular, but they hardly refer to "it." "These atrocities made . . ." clears the reference.

> Vicki Biehn Swan has traveled extensively to exotic places, has read all the classics—some twice—frequents lectures at Yale whenever a person of importance is scheduled, and runs fifteen miles a day. This keeps her mind alert.

The word "This" just does not fit. It generally refers to all of Vicki's activities. The writer needs to replace "This" with something like "These stimulations."

NUMBER TWO: USING THE WRONG CASE FOR PRONOUNS, INCLUDING WHO AND WHOM

Every morning I listen to the *Today* Show on NBC. When Matt and Katie go after some of the interviewees, those questioned sometimes forget what proper speech is. For example, on June 10, 2004, Michael Cordoza, a lawyer involved with the Scott Peterson case, ended one of his sentences with the following:

> ". . . talked about *he* and his wife."

Then a week later, Catherine Crier (also involved in the same case) ended one of her sentences with

> ". . . conversations between *he* and Amy."

In both examples, "he" should be "him." The grammatical ruling is that the objective case (see Appendix One for a complete list of pronouns) must be used because the pronoun is the object of the preposition (see Chapter Two). Had the speakers thought about what they were saying, and I realize that during an interview there is little time for analysis, they would never have made that mistake. Mr. Cordoza, had he dropped "his wife" (not literally, of course), would never say "talked about he" because, for one thing, it just does not sound right. For another, a pronoun used as the object of the preposition must be in the objective case.

On June 10, 2004, Bill O'Reilly, in speaking about former President Reagan, said the following:

> ". . . who we do respect . . ."

Mr. O'Reilly certainly has enough airtime and has written enough to know the difference between *who* and *whom*. And the producers of the old TV show *Who Do You Trust?* Should not they have known that the proper word was "whom"?

Now, if this criticism sounds like nitpicking, answer the phone next time and say, "It is I." The person calling will hang up because she has the wrong number. "It's me!" is grammatically incorrect but socially acceptable.

NUMBER THREE: THE MISUSE OF IRREGULAR VERBS (MIXING UP THE PAST AND THE PAST PARTICIPLE)

My awareness of the misuse of irregular forms of verbs started in the bowling alley. As one of my teammates returned to his seat after wobbling the tenpin left standing, he muttered, "It should have *went.*"

As the only English teacher on the team, I corrected him by saying, "gone." There is no need to repeat his comment, but at least he knew that his choice of words ruffled my feathers. In addition, I've heard aberrations such as "tooken," "wroten," "brung," and "done" in the place of *did;* not always do I correct, especially if the speaker is bigger than I am.

The following examples point out the misuse of several verb parts. (For a complete listing of the irregular verbs, see Appendix Three.) In each sentence, the corrected form follows the mistake.

1. Don Williams *casted* (cast) toward the ripple in the water.

2. Deshond Griffin should have *took* (taken) her mentor's advice about her resume.

3. Bob Schumann, had he *drank* (drunk) more water, would not be dehydrated.

4. Jack O'Connor said that he had *ate* (eaten) too much at Chipper's picnic.
5. Without thinking, Thomas Brusnicki Wilson had *tore* (torn) his rotator cuff while fixing his chainsaw.
6. Hugh Currie hurt his hand after he had *wrote* (written) a hundred Christmas cards.
7. If Jack Law had *swam* (swum) faster, he would have avoided arrest.
8. Apparently Susan Terese Reily thought the magician had *sawed* (sawn) the lady in two.
9. Ron Nophsker thought he should have *spoke* (spoken) more clearly while giving directions to the stranger.
10. (Heard on the *Jerry Springer* Show) My husband should never have *forgave* (forgiven) me.

How do these mistakes occur? Is it necessary to memorize the list of irregular verbs (see Appendix Three) to avoid making mistakes like the above? Perhaps to have command of any language, there should be some sort of memorization so that the bugaboos become known and then not used in formal, and even in informal, speaking or writing.

THEN SOME . . .

Whom or Who?

At a party once, Chip Stone asked John Bush (George W. Bush's uncle) a poser using "whoever" or "whomever" as in the following:

> Phyllis Abeel Lennon asked (whoever, whomever) was involved in the controversy at the Ocean View Club to come forward for reprimand.

Without hesitation, Mr. Bush said, "Whoever because it is the subject of the noun clause and must be in the subjective case." And then he added, "At Yale, one had to know grammar."

Certainly colleges and universities are concerned with grammar and, of course, with the correct choices between *who* and *whom* and *whoever* and *whomever*. Why then are mistakes made every day somewhere? Why do many speakers and writers "settle" for *who* in almost every case simply because *whom* is not part of their vocabulary? Rhetorical questions aside, why not go back with me for a moment to fifth grade when Miss Mary O'Brien taught the difference between subjects and objects. Distinguishing between *who* and *whom* became second nature then.

"*Who* is used as the subject or predicate pronoun of a sentence or clause and *whom* is used as the object of the verb or preposition," she intoned in her singsong voice. This topic was simple because if students did not learn this bit of grammar, they found themselves in the same seat, same grade, the following year. Even in the 1940s, unwritten policy said that no child would be left behind—as long as that student knew the difference between subjective and objective case.

Take the following test and then check your answers in Appendix Ten. Once you have read the explanations, you should have a good idea of how to use *who* or *whom*, *whoever* or *whomever*.

1. (Who, Whom) did Mary Jane Fegen say was the best patient at Rehab Concepts?

2. (Who, Whom) did the best artwork at the latest Daniel Hand Art Show?

3. If you had to choose the best student in the school, (who, whom) would it be?

4. The scholarship was granted to (whoever, whomever) maintained perfect attendance.

5. Steve Lynch hired (whoever, whomever) he thought best at building daiquiris.

6. Steve Lynch hired (whoever, whomever) was the best at making daiquiris.

7. The Major League catcher hitting the most home runs is (who, whom)?

8. Get (who, whom) you will to fill the position of dog-catcher.

9. Ray Charles once said that he would talk to (whoever, whomever) would listen.

10. (Who, whom) do you trust?

Lie or Lay?

Why not start this discussion with the principal parts of the two verbs and the definitions?

> *Lay, laid, laid, laying*—to put or set down; to place for rest or sleep
>
> *Lie, lay, lain, lying*—to assume a horizontal position; to be prostrate; to rest or recline
>
> *Lie, lied, lied, lying*—to tell a whopper, to fib

How many times have you heard someone say

> I feel ill; I'm going to *lay* down.

> *or*

> Things are getting too close. I'd better *lay* low.

Both examples contain mistakes because in the first one the speaker might be assuming a horizontal position, while the second speaker, although not really resting, seems to think he should remain quiet (i.e., lie) than do anything else.

Another way to avoid mixing these up is to remember that *lay* (present tense) can take an object as in the following:

> Mary Beth Simmons should *lay* the package (direct object) on the table before opening the door.

On the other hand, when one is talking about resting, *lie* is the correct response as in the following:

> Janice Schneider thought I should *lie* (no object) down because of my condition.

In Chapter Fourteen, you can try your hand at all sorts of usage problems, along with other errors in writing and speaking.

Like or As (If)?

Did the mix-up of *like* and *as* (*if*) stem from "Winston tastes good like a cigarette should"? Probably not. However, we know for a fact that the word *like* has crept into our language in a way not intended by lexographers.

Like you know what I'm talking about *like* . . .

More precisely, *like* is a preposition, and *as* is a conjunction. *Like* introduces a phrase, while *as* introduces a clause:

> <u>Like a pig</u>, Carl Raudat ate the pizza, snorting all the time. (prepositional phrase)
>
> Jackie Robinson played baseball <u>as if he *were* possessed</u>. (adverb clause with a subject and verb italicized)

Notice what happens when we misuse these words:

> Gil Hodges swept up errant throws *like* a vacuum cleaner sucked up scattered mouse droppings.

Actually nothing happens! IT SOUNDS RIGHT! Of course, it should read ". . . as a vacuum cleaner sucked up . . . ." Here's another example:

> Like I said, perhaps you, Bobby Bushnell, should look for other employment.

What's wrong here? Nothing, according to modern usage, because few care about precise language enough to write about it or use it correctly or . . . . However, we know that the clause should read "As I said . . . ." BUT THAT SOUNDS WRONG!

And then I was surfing for high and low tides for the upcoming week of fishing and chanced upon *stripersonline.com*:

"Striped bass and surf fishing info <u>like</u> you've never seen before! [Author's underscore]

Of course, *as* would sound wrong.

You're and Your

How simple are these two words! *You're* is a contraction for "you are," while *your* indicates a possessive. There should be no problem whatsoever with *yours*. However, in *USA Today* an ad about timeshares ran under the title "TIMESHARE RESALE." The first question asked: "Tired of Not Getting The Exchanges <u>Your</u> Used To?" ("Your should be "You're." I'll not mention the mistakes with capital letters.)

Their, They're, and There

"They" are all pronounced the same. "They" all begin with the first three letters "the," so that the difficulty stems from writing usage. Use them in one sentence and see the difference:

They're there with their families.

Perhaps a strategy is appropriate. Eliminate one by pointing at some object and say, "There!" the pointing, the direction, the "there" ingredients, stand out. This logic leaves only *they're* and *their*. Let's go further: "Their" has the same two vowels as "friends," only reversed. "Their friends," then, triggers correctness. The contraction remains. "They're" can be eliminated from the consideration if you write and speak without contractions like *don't*, *won't*, and *shouldn't* (or like Emily Dickinson's "did'nt"). If you must use *they're*, just know that it means "they are."

Best advice: Just learn them, and as the Beatles intoned, "Let it be. Let it be."

Its and It's

It's own stable door

If students of mine ever wrote something like the line above, they would have been subject to public humiliation (kidding, of course), but not one of them wrote it—Emily Dickinson did. Her intention? My guess is that because she wrote mostly for herself (only about seven of her poems were published during her lifetime), she could not have cared less about following certain rules. Anyone else using "it's" for "its" stands out like a sore thumb.

Its: Neuter possessive
The tree shed <u>its</u> leaves in three days.
The brook babbled <u>its</u> song endlessly.
It's: A contraction for it is.
<u>It's</u> raining, <u>it's</u> pouring, the old man . . . .
<u>It's</u> a great day in Boston anytime they win.

There's nothing really difficult about this mistake, yet why do many beginning writers make it?

Imply and Infer

Imply (*implying, implied, implication*) means to hint at something, to suggest without stating literally. An implication comes from a speaker, a writer, or an actor (not necessarily on stage, either).

When Bill Alberino warned his students to study for hours for the final exam, he *implied* the test would be difficult.

> As Bruce Keeton walked into Lynch's with a dejected look, he *implied* that he had shot another bad round of golf.

Infer (*inferring, inferred, inference*) means to draw a conclusion, to deduce from what was said, written, or acted.

> When Joe Gallagher wrinkled his nose at her food order, Maggie Driscoll Floyd *inferred* that she should try something else.

> Deborah Ramsay McGuire was *inferring* that her husband did not want to rake leaves because when she asked him to help, he started rubbing his arms and groaning.

These two words fit almost into the active/passive mode, *imply* the active (the speaker, the writer, the actor) and *infer* the passive (the listener, the reader, the audience). Years ago, Jane Austen used these words interchangeably because at that time (nineteenth century) they were interchangeable. Now, even on the SAT Reading Comprehension section, students will find questions like "What does the author *imply* . . . ?" and "From what the author poses, what can the reader *infer* from . . . ?"

The rest of those confused and misused words the reader can find in Chapter Eight. Check Appendix Six for current examples of language goofs committed by those who should know better.

Ideals are the Fairy Oil
With which we help the Wheel
Emily Dickinson

Chapter Eight

WORDS CONFUSED AND MISUSED AND ABUSED

"I'm at the peak of pique."

Many English words cause confusion because of either spelling or pronunciation or both. For example, *accept* and *except* are not supposed to be pronounced the same, but since most of us do, when it comes time for the writer to use either one, a scratching of the head occurs: Which is which? Also, *should of* comes from the pronunciation of "should've," the latter the correct version, but beginning writers will use the former version. *Supposively* is incorrect as is *suppose to* even *supposebly* probably because of *supposive* and the *t* sound from the *to*. *Supposedly* and *supposed to* are the correct items; *supposebly* does not exist.

Sailors developed shortenings of words even though in the old days voyages sometimes lasted years, but tars insisted the *forecastle* be pronounced "fo'c'sle," and *gunwale*, "gun'l." Even in regattas, a *coxswain* is a "coc's'n," a man is an oar, and once in a while a rower "catches a crab," when the oar is out of sync with the rhythm of the cadence. These examples, however, are not incorrect, just different. And then there's the word *victuals*, which is pronounced to rhyme with "spittles."

Most of the following words have been misused over the centuries, and some even have changed in meaning. These facts, difficult to understand perhaps, nevertheless plague beginning speakers and writers and those who should know better. One of the English teachers on our staff pronounced *asterisk* as "asterik"—no second *s*. I often think that maybe I should have steered him right, and as I was thinking that thought the other day and listening to *Mike and the Mad Dog* on Fan Radio, Mike Francessa said "asterik." I was going to call in to correct him too, but I feared being interrupted. Then the next day with Imus interviewing Phil Simms, Imus was talking about his producer who could not find "this cut of you [Simms] and I." Perhaps it is better to be thought of as stupid than to open your mouth and remove all doubt.

USAGE

A, an, the Use *a* before a consonant SOUND; use *an* before a vowel SOUND; use *the*, a definite article, before any noun that is particular rather than generic. The question arises: What do I use in front of "historic," *a* or *an*? Experts agree on *an* because the *h* is in the unaccented syllable and therefore almost sounds like a vowel.

> Bob and Stephanie Nilson love to go on **a** picnic.
>
> Steve, Lauren, Megan, and Brandon Geary own **an** original copy of *How to Teach Little Leaguers How to Hit*, written by their father.
>
> Judith Adams wrote **the** book, *How to Avoid Sweeping Generalizations*.
>
> David Arnold Graham and John Daniel Hardy consider the demise of the Holy Roman Empire **an** historic series of events.

Absolutely Do not use *absolutely*, absolutely.

Abstemious, arsenious, facetious The only three words in the English language that have all the vowels in order. If *y* is considered a vowel, nothing changes in adverb forms of these words: *abstemiously, arseniously, facetiously*.

Accede, exceed If you *accede* to (something), you agree to (a pact, a contract) and become a part of it. *Exceed* means that you are superior to or go beyond a certain established point. Also, consider the synonyms: *surpass, transcend, excel, outdo,* and *outstrip,* which all mean going beyond a certain point, limit, measure, or degree—stated or implied.

The new engine in my old boat **exceeded** my expectations.

When Bob Wigham told me I should stick with a gas engine instead of diesel, I **acceded**.

Accept, except As discussed in the introduction to this chapter concerning the way words are spoken, the confusion here definitely results from pronunciation. Said quickly, both these words sound the same because of the unaccented vowels in the first syllable. Also, in the usual context, the first is a verb and the second a preposition. However, *except* can be used as a verb.

Accept (verb)—to receive willingly; to believe; to endure without protest

Lana Reich **accepted** the responsibility of feeding the cats of the Ariston Hotel.

Except (preposition)—not including

Rosemarie Whitford has flown on every airline **except** Spirit.

Except (verb)—to omit or leave out

As Joe Bruno listed the best teams ever in the Major Leagues, he **excepted** the New York Mets because he said they have been too inconsistent to be great.

Adapt, adopt, adept The first, *adapt*, means to make fit, to alter as to fit. People can adapt to an environment (make themselves "fit" the surroundings); when Americans go abroad, they bring adaptors, portable contraptions that allow electrical devices rated 110 to "adapt" to the European 220.

The second, *adopt*, means to take as one's own. You can adopt a child or you can adopt someone else's thoughts and make them your own.

The third, *adept*, means skillful and really is never confused with the other two. One can be adept with the mind or the body, and that's enough of that.

Adverse, averse The adjective *adverse* means hostile, unfavorable, or harmful. The adjective *averse* means having an active repugnance for, or disinclined.

> Because of the **adverse** weather, the soccer game was rescheduled.

> Robert Dewitt Vosburgh was **averse** to patronizing Lynch's because Dan the bartender bothered him.

Affect, effect Mixed up because of pronunciation, these two words seem to find their way into almost every standardized test. Also, both can be used as two distinct parts of speech:

> **Affect** (verb)—to influence

> When star athletes use steroids, beginning players are **affected**.

> **Affect** (noun)—the conscious subjective aspect of an emotion

> Dr. Mark Catania's patients show remarkable **affects** after his secret treatments.

> **Effect** (noun)—a result

> Lisa Judith Valentine has a profound **effect** on everyone she meets.

> **Effect** (verb)—to cause or bring about

> Jonathan Harris Vosburgh **effected** a deal that made his family wealthy.

Affluence, effluence While *affluence* means wealth, it also means an influx, a flowing in. One can readily see that these two words might sometimes be confused because *effluence* means a flowing out.

> The Hammonasset River's **effluence** continues through Clinton Harbor.
>
> The Hammonasset River's **affluence** takes more than six hours.
>
> Joe Gallagher's **affluence** is exceeded only by his good looks.

Aggravate I heard this statement the other day: "If you don't stop **aggravating** me, I'll scream." I thought *aggravate* meant to make worse or to intensify negatively, and *Webster's Collegiate* backed me up. However, the use of *aggravating* in the example sentence is correct; moreover, if you run on a treadmill, you are likely to **aggravate** the hamstring injury.

Allude, refer When authors allude to something, they refer indirectly to a person, place, thing, or idea. When they refer specifically to an item, they are direct in their reference.

> As Stephanie Nilson discussed the Green Bay Packers, she **alluded** to the cheeseheads as "obnoxious." (She made an indirect reference to the Packer fans.)
>
> As Stephanie Nilson discussed the Green Bay Packers, she **referred** to their fans as "obnoxious."

Allusion, illusion An *allusion* is an indirect reference, while an *illusion* is a mistaken idea.

> Edith Wharton in *Ethan Frome* makes **allusions** to the emptiness of the winter environment by naming Ethan's town Starkfield.
>
> Some fighters create the **illusion** of sluggishness to lure their opponents into carelessness.

A lot, alot In formal writing, unless you are a real estate agent, avoid either form.

Already, all ready The first is an adverb:

> Kathy Doonan **already** purchased Red Sox season tickets.

But the second means a group of things at the quick:

> The Yankees seem **all ready** to contend once again for the league championship.

Alright, all right When I went to school, the use of *alright* meant points off on quizzes and tests. Now, *alright* seems to find its way into business journals and dialogue in fiction.

> "**Alright**, I'll go," said Lenny to George.
>
> When the Mets win the pennant, everything is **all right** in my world.

Alumnus, alumni, alumna, alumnae With most schools coed these days, perhaps the second two will not appear as readily as before. However, purists will always hold that

> **Alumnus** means a male graduate.
>
> **Alumni** means male or female graduates of a coed school.
>
> **Alumna** means a female graduate.
>
> **Alumnae** means many female graduates.

Amount, number Sometimes these are used interchangeably but not correctly, of course. *Amount* is a singular unit and accompanies singular words. *Number* is also a singular word but accompanies plural words.

Omar Francis said that the **amount** of money one makes can pave the way on the road to financial security.

Donna Francis, on the other hand, said that the **number** of bills in one's wallet is the key to success. (nice assumption)

Note: Even though the word used with *number* may not look plural, that is, without an *s* at the end, *number* is correct:

Number of people, **number** of deer, **number** of children, **number** of phenomena

Anecdote, antidote An *anecdote* is a short amusing, sometimes interesting, sometimes biographical story. An *antidote* is what one takes to relieve symptoms of poison or something that counteracts a negative. Some interesting offshoots of the first:

Anecdotage—old age garrulity

Anecdotalist—one skilled in telling anecdotes

Len Lonnegren loves to tell **anecdotes** about his life in Sweden.

And etc. Etc., an abbreviation for *et cetera—et* means and; *cetera* means so on. *And etc.,* therefore, is redundant.

Any more, anymore As two words, *any more* is an adjective *any* and a pronoun *more.* As one word, *anymore* is an adverb and means any longer or at the present time.

Carolyn Ann Eltzholtz said that she did not have **any more** business cards available.

Patricia Clark Harvey refuses to ride the subway **anymore** in New York.

Nancy Murphy Wilson said that she hoped the rain would not upset her plans **anymore** today.

ATM machine Modern redundancy. The M in ATM means machine.

Auger, augur An *auger* bores holes (Ask any ice fisherman); an *augur* is either one who can tell future events based on certain omens or the sign of the future itself. The confusion mostly is in the spelling because both words are pronounced the same.

> The **auger** used on Candlewood Lake bore a hole six inches in diameter.

> The **augur** predicted strange occurrences based on the cloud formation.

Avocation, vocation Some dictionaries tell us that these two words are synonyms meaning occupation. However, religious orders are still considered *vocations*, while *avocations* are hobbies. Regular work, according to the purist, is a *vocation*.

Axt, asked At the risk of offending some of my friends who should know better:

> When you **asked** (not *axt*) me for a favor . . .

> When Andrew James Doonan **asked** (not *axt*) his father if the Red Sox would win the World Series again, Greg Doonan smiled dreamily.

Basically Basically, *basically* is one of those words writers do not need.

Bazaar, bizarre Pronunciation trouble again—which leads to spelling problems. A *bazaar* is a department store, nowadays, but in the past, and in certain countries now, a market with stalls selling all sorts of things. A *bizarre* occurrence is one that is odd or fantastic. A *bizarre* is also a flower with striped markings that border on the eccentric, but I have never seen one.

Because, reason These two words should never be used in the same sentence like the following because they essentially mean the same thing:

> The **reason** that Dana Marie Supeau moved to California was **because** she disliked the wine made in Connecticut.

There are two ways to correct this egregious error:

> The **reason** . . . was **that** . . .
> The **reason** . . . was . . .

Because of, due to *Because of* means on account of or by reason of. *Due to* is often used as a synonym for *because of.*

> **Correct: Because of** circumstances beyond her control, Kathryn Frances Connor McNulty promptly cut the lines of the sailing craft and watched it drift away.

> **Correct: Due to** the lack of funds, our library closed.

> **Better: Because of** the lack of funds, our library closed.

Where these two differ is in the other definitions of *due to:* owing or payable to, as in

> "Lynch's bartenders were given the money **due to** them."

Due to also means announced as or likely to.

> We bought more of Abbot stock because Charles Schwab said it was **due to** rise.

In these cases, *because of* cannot be substituted.

Being as, being that; seeing as, seeing that In formal speaking and writing, these pairs are never used. Use *since* or *because* instead.

> **Wrong: Seeing as** Tyler James Wilson did tricks on a skateboard; he was asked to participate in the X-games in Newport.
>
> **Correct: Because** Tyler . . .
>
> **Wrong: Being as** Ron Prior was voted "Personality of the year," his boss doubled his salary.
>
> **Correct: Since** Ron . . .

Beside, besides *Beside* means next to; *besides* means in addition to or furthermore and is a preposition. *Besides* is three parts of speech:

> **Preposition: Besides** being practical, Winfred Scofield Berlt is generous.
>
> **Adverb: Besides**, Bruce Llewelyan Berlt spends money as if it's going out of style.
>
> **Adjective:** The **besides** factor figures in most decisions that have many alternatives.

Between, among In the 1950s, Brother Jerome at Notre Dame High School in West Haven, Connecticut, taught that there should be no problem learning these two words. "Use *between* to separate two items; use *among* (never *amongst*) to separate three or more items." Well, sorry, Brother . . . .

Even when there are several items mentioned:

> NATO helped to establish ground rules for discussion **between** Russia, France, Germany, and the United States.

Also, if items are spelled out:

> **Between** you and me and the groundhogs, I do not care if I see my shadow anytime.

Furthermore, if the items are not listed, but rather lumped into a plural noun:

> In 2005, National Hockey League owners could not decide **between** them what was best for the league.

Two items:

> Billy Patrick Contois jumped **between** the two Cadillacs to avoid getting thumped by the dirt bike.
>
> Erik Francis Leon Hesselberg settled the argument **among** the reporters by dictating certain usage rules.

Bring, take Two more words on almost every usage test known to students. *Bring* means going toward the speaker, as in: **Bring** me the newspaper. *Take*, on the other hand, means going away from the speaker, as in: **Take** this newspaper to your father.

> Jonathan Thomas Wilson **took** his lunch to school.
>
> Tucker Nolan Wilson **brought** his lunch home.

Buck naked, butt naked I'll wager most would choose the latter as correct; they would err. *Buck* conjures up a knife but also means completely or stark.

Capital, capitol In 1950, we learned in Mr. Walter C. "Pop" Polson's class that Hartford, the *capital* of Connecticut had a building in it with a dome, which is round "like a circle" and therefore spelled with an *o*, as in *capitol*. Also, as a noun, *capital* meant money or the uppermost part of a column.

The protestors gathered outside the **capitol** in downtown Hartford.

Many of Dillon Robert Wilson's ideas are based on **capital** gains.

Carat, karat, caret, carrot *Carat* or *karat* both mean the weight of precious gems or metals. In magazine ads, one will find *carat* when the word is spelled, but abbreviated one will see, for example, "24K" to indicate the weight. A *caret*, on the other hand, is a wedge-like mark (^) used to indicate that a word is missing in a sentence. *Carrot*, pronounced just like the other three, is the orange root that is good for you.

Cite, sight, site Again, the pronunciation leads to error. If you *cite* something, you quote it verbatim or refer to something written or spoken, but if you are *cited*, you must appear before a court. *Site* has an old meaning that means a place where a house or other buildings are located; the new meaning applies to the Internet as in web site. *Site* can also be used as a verb meaning locate or place in a certain position. A *sight* is a spectacle or something seen; a "**sight** for sore eyes" is a well-known cliché.

Cliché A *cliché* is a word, phrase, clause, or sentence that is so trite as to be meaningless. "You make a better door than a window (even though you are a 'pane.')"; "ugly as sin." Get the idea? Here are six more:

> Can of worms
> Like it's going out of style
> In harm's way
> Can't teach an old dog new tricks
> Handle with kid gloves
> Even a blind squirrel finds an acorn occasionally
> Slow as molasses in January

Want one more? Variety is the spice of life!

Climactic, climatic Those careful with pronunciation will never mix up these two. The first, *climactic*, comes from *climax*, that point of highest interest in a story, long or short. *Climatic*'s base word is *climate*—relating to weather.

> The **climactic** scene in *Of Mice and Men*, where Lenny Small unwittingly shakes Curley's wife to death, causes the reader to pity both the attacker and the victim.

> The **climatic** change from heat to cold affected the orange crop in Sicily.

Complement, compliment

Complement—the quantity, number, or assortment that makes something complete or to make something complete:

> Mark Twain once said that he **complemented** his wife. She knew all there was to know, and he knew all the rest.

Compliment—to praise or show favor to. A complimentary ticket is one given freely perhaps as a favor:

> When we would visit Coach Lenny Wilkens at Madison Square Garden, he would give us **complimentary** tickets to that night's game.

Continual, continuous *Continual* hints at prolonged succession or recurrence, while *continuous* suggests an uninterrupted flow or space extension.

> The **continual** snow during the weekend prevented us from driving to Vermont.

> One of Sicily's **continuous** traditions is the giving of gifts—not on Christmas but on All Souls' Eve.

Could of, would of, should of, must of, might of These constructions do not exist. The *-ve* represents the sound of "of" and therefore the mistake. If writers never abbreviated, they would not run into these problems.

Council, counsel, consul A *council* is a gathering for the purpose of discussion, consultation, or agreement. Also, it can be used as an adjective referring to Native American business.

> The **council** met to determine whether Mayor Tom Rylander actually proposed a week-long holiday for everyone in Madison who played golf.

> The **council** area crowded fast as issues flew back and forth.

A *counsel* is advice given or giving or the lawyer in a certain court case.

> The **counsel** of the teacher warned the unruly student about behavior in the hallway.

> The **counsel** for the defense recommended the death penalty for Scott Peterson.

A *consul* is an appointee to a certain country to represent commercial interests of the appointing country.

> The **consul** at the American Embassy in Paris strongly criticized France's behavior after 9/11.

Credible (incredible), credulous (incredulous), creditable A *credible* testimony is believable, just as an *incredible* testimony is not believable. However, the word *incredible* has lately become an interjection for any different situation:

> **Incredible!** If I were not there, I would not have thought the Red Sox could actually win the World Series.

A *credulous* person sometimes is referred to as gullible, but if you look closely at the definition, he is anything but gullible. *Credulous* means believing something based on very little evidence; *trusting* might be a better synonym. An *incredulous* person is skeptical about something, not convinced about the verity of the subject.

Creditable has nothing to do with either one of the above. *Creditable* means praiseworthy:

> When Makenzie Shannon Lynch did such a **creditable** job waitressing for the first time, she was elevated to hostess immediately.

Criterion, criteria The first one is singular and the second plural.

> Jack O'Malley Lynch's **criterion** for a good hamburger is it must have a one-inch slice of vadalia onion.

> Judy Camp's **criteria** for a good vacation spot are (plural verb for plural subject) an Olympic size pool, plenty of shopping nearby, restaurants within walking distance, and an extra tough chaise lounge for her husband, Wall.

Data, datum A big change of meaning for these two, according to *Webster's Collegiate*, Edition Eleven: *Data* in modern usage can serve both as a singular and a plural, whereas in the past it was always plural. As a plural, that which most publishers will insist on, *data* (like facts) takes a plural verb (*data are, data were stored*) and is referred to by plural pronouns (*these, them*). *Data* also can be singular (*data is, data was stored*) and is referred to by a singular pronoun (*it*) when it means a mass of facts, like information. *Datum*, I guess, will always remain singular and mean "one piece of information" or "fact."

Defuse, diffuse If you wish to make a bomb, or anything dangerous less dangerous, you would *defuse* it. If you wish to scatter seed or information, you would *diffuse* it. Also, if you throw words around carelessly and redundantly (like the last eight words), you could be thought of as *diffuse* (wordy to the *n*th degree and extremely disorganized).

Desert, dessert First, "<u>s</u>econd <u>s</u>erving" is a tricky way to remember the last course of a meal. A *desert* (noun) is an arid **tract** of land as in Egypt. Also, *desert* is an adjective as in *desert* outpost or sparsely populated, abandoned. Furthermore, *desert* (noun) means deserved reward or punishment or even worth or excellence. Finally, *desert* (verb) means to abandon, or to withdraw from or leave with no intention of returning.

> Tess Alexandra Lynch said that in the **desert,** going from one dried up rill to another was like going from one ex-stream to another.

> Johanna Catharina Cashman once spent a year on a **desert** island.

> To **desert** one's post in warfare is to commit a serious crime.

Different from, different than *From* is a preposition and introduces a phrase (a group of words with no verb); *than* is an adverbial conjunction introducing a clause (See Chapter Three).

> Kathleen Lynch once said that Ireland was **different from** anywhere <u>else</u> in the world. (object of the preposition)

> "When I visited the Vatican," said Connor Lynch, "it was **different than** <u>I had imagined</u>." (clause)

Dis, disrespect *Dis* (also *diss*), *dissed, dissing* made it into *Webster's Collegiate* as slang, meaning to disrespect or to criticize.

Disc, disk *Disc* has a label, "usu," which means usually. The usual definition of *disc*, then, has to do with computers and music, while *disk* means the central part of a flower, the part of the spinal column that slips or a star or solar disk. However, *Webster's Collegiate* equates the two words.

Discreet, discrete To be *discreet* is showing good judgment, being prudent, or being unpretentious or modest. *Discrete*, on the other hand, means distinct.

> Cristine Elizabeth Hine showed she was **discreet** by ignoring the unruly diner.

> Richard Kirst made himself famous by constructing **discrete** housing in several neighborhoods.

Disinterested, uninterested Many use these words interchangeably, but *disinterested* means not having the mind or feelings working or unbiased. *Uninterested* connotes that the mind might be otherwise occupied.

> Peter Andrew Lynch seemed **disinterested** in the present conversation because he was concentrating on the lamb chops on his plate.

> Stacy Alex Lynch once said, "I am **uninterested** in playing basketball because softball is the only game."

Double negatives The modern rule states that two negatives are incorrect and that there are words that are obviously negative: *none, not, n't, never, nothing, no one, nobody*; also, there are those not so negative: *hardly, scarcely, barely, but*, but still negative. Like in math, two negatives make a positive; in English, two negatives also create a positive: To say, "I ai**n't** got **none**" means that really you have some!

Double: Dr. J. Kevin Lynch told me after my double knee replacement, "If the world were flat you would**n't** have **nothing** to worry about."

Double: Sedona Leach heard her teacher say that homework is **hardly never** the answer to scholarship.

Correct: Daniel Leach vowed **never** to go swimming without a life preserver.

Correct: Nina Clark **scarcely** looks up as she bones a cooler full of shad filets.

Note: Here is a double negative that even sounds correct: "I can't help **but** think that the Waldorf Astoria has better food than the Monkey Farm," mused Deb Corning. ("Can't help thinking that . . ." would be the correct way.)

Dual, duel The first one indicates two of something, like *dual* exhaust. The second, *duel*, is two opponents fighting, sometimes with swords, sometimes with words.

Elicit, illicit To **elicit** an **illicit** response . . . . *Elicit* means to draw forth, as a response or a thought. *Illicit* means unlawful or not permitted.

Ms. Secondi **elicited** quick responses from her eighth grade English class.

Some of Mr. Kieffer's students sobbed after caught committing **illicit** acts in the hallway.

Emigrate, immigrate (emigrant, immigrant) When people *emigrate*, they leave a country to settle elsewhere. When they *immigrate*, the come into a country to settle there. From those definitions, one can see how an *emigrant* and *immigrant* could be the same person, depending on perspective.

When my grandmother Nana Mulvey **emigrated** from Ireland, she settled in New Haven, just off Whaley Avenue.

When Anna Sheehan Schubert **immigrated** to America, she traveled across the Atlantic by herself at eighteen.

Eminent, immanent, imminent *Eminent* means conspicuous, projecting, prominent, or famous. *Immanent* means inherent or being within one's knowledge or experience. *Imminent* means about to happen or ready to take place.

Ward Churchill, a once **eminent** professor at the University of Colorado, was asked to resign because of some insensitive remarks concerning victims of 9/11.

His **immanent** knowledge of the occult made John Thomas Lynch famous.

As Kaitlin Lynch looked out her kitchen window, she noticed the dark clouds and told everyone in the household there was a major winter storm **imminent**.

Empathy, sympathy (empathize, sympathize, empathetic, sympathetic) *Empathy*, if one has it, is an understanding of someone else's feelings without experiencing those feelings personally. *Sympathy*, on the other hand, is more of pity or attraction since the person sympathizing may actually experience the other's feelings.

Not too many baseball fans **empathize** with Barry Bonds, mostly because of his behavior off the field.

Millions **sympathize** with parents of soldiers killed in Iraq.

Ensure, insure, assure, secure *Ensure*, a product of Abbot Labs, uses the brand name "guarantee" for seniors to make sure they receive proper nutrition. *Insure* implies a protection, or guarantee beforehand. *Assure* means that whatever the situation, the doubt or uncertainty will be removed. *Secure* implies protection against some kind of attack, mental or physical.

> Jeffrey John Manning installed an alarm system to **ensure** that his mansion would not be violated.
>
> Elizabeth Jo Manning decided to **insure** the mansion by doubling the premium on both mansion and property.
>
> Sara Jo Manning **assured** her mom that staying out late was not the plan.
>
> Joseph John Manning felt **secure** in the mansion with the armed guard out front.

Envelop, envelope Clearly, these words, although looking alike, differ both in meaning and in pronunciation. In fact, if one now pronounces the beginning of *envelope* to rhyme with "on," he would be accused, although accepted, of sounding pseudo-French. The standard American pronunciation of the beginning of *envelope* should sound just like the letter *n*. *Envelop* is a verb which means to surround completely or mount an attack on the flank of an enemy.

> In the **envelope** was the name of the actor who had won the award for best actor.
>
> Cassandra Beth Day **enveloped** the toy poodle after it had been hit by the moped.

Farther, further Used interchangeably for years, this "Siamese" pair now shows signs of being separated, once and for all. For anything involving distance, *farther* is the logical choice. If there is no hint of distance, use *further*.

Kerin Donovan Raftery lives **farther** from Madison than does Cortney Paige Worthy.

Elijah Bruce Harvey **further** stated that his English teacher in high school promised him a fishing trip but never delivered.

Furthermore, furthermore, serves as an effective transitional expression either at the beginning of a sentence or right after a semicolon:

Furthermore, . . .

; furthermore,

Formally, formerly *Formally*, that is in a formal manner, and *formerly*, that is in the past, are related only in the first four letters.

Jane Clink **formally** proposed to her editors that her writing was perfect and needed no changes.

Ron Clink, **formerly** of the corporate world, became Professor of Economics at the University of Cincinnati.

Good, well *Good* is an adjective. *Well* is an adverb. How do you feel? If it's *good*, you're healthy. If it's *well*, you have an extraordinary sense of touch.

The eggplant that Helen Lockhart makes is so **good** that it rivals any recipe in the world.

Mickey Hawkes does everything so **well** that he defies all odds.

Note: **Good** can also function as a noun:

Tim Flood, during his forty years as a teacher, did so much **good** that he was voted Teacher of the Century.

Had ought to, hadn't ought to Use just *ought* or *should.*

> Wendy Gifford said that I **should** (not *had ought to*) read more to realize my potential.

> Bobby Nilson recommended that Corey **should not** (not *hadn't ought to*) go fishing with Dan Mulvey because the latter did not know what he was doing.

Hanged, hung Once, in Father McGregor's sophomore English class at Providence College, I was docked twenty points for mixing up these two words. The answer to the question was "He was hanged." I had written, "He was hung." End of conversation.

Pictures, drapes, plants are *hung.* Criminals and witches are *hanged.*

> According to rumors surrounding the Salem witch trials, those suspected of witchcraft were burned at the stake; however, history tells us that that they were **hanged**, not burned.

> As Elisabeth Anna Clink intoned, "The stockings were **hung** by the chimney with care," Maggie Jane Clink and Hannah Rose Clink both puddled up and asked for handkerchiefs.

> Barnette Dwain Grayer got to know several of the Chicago Bulls when they **hung** around the Hotel Monaco.

Hisself, theirselves No such words. Use *himself* and *themselves. Ourself* might seem haughty, but it is correct usage, while with *ourselves*, there is no confusion. Macbeth said he would "keep **ourself** till supper time alone." I never argue with Shakespeare.

Impact I thought for years that *impact* as a verb is pretentious. I have changed my mind. In fact, I am in awe of the various forms of the word and once had an *impacted* wisdom tooth by which to remember the word. Forms include *impactful, impactive,* **impactor**

(also, *impacter*), and *impaction*. Ralph Waldo Emerson said that it was justified to change one's mind on occasions.

Imply, infer See Chapter Seven.

Infamous, notorious If one is *infamous*, he is disgraceful, but not necessarily widely known. If a person is *notorious*, he is widely known for the wrong things.

> In our old neighborhood, one of our friends became **infamous** for letting his dogs roam at will.
>
> Sal "The Barber" Maglie, the **notorious** shaver of the Brooklyn Dodgers, thought nothing of throwing at batters' heads.

Internet, web site *Internet* is always capitalized, although *web site* is not.

> The **Internet** comprises huge numbers of **web sites**.

Kudos, Kudo A *kudos* (singular) is praise for work well done. *Kudo* does not exist.

> Jason Scott Aubrey received **kudos** from body building magazines for his outstanding rehabilitation of Kevin Walsh.

Lay, lie See Chapter Seven.

Leave, let *Let* is to allow or to rent. *Leave* means that you are going away. The only time these two are interchangeable is in the following sentences:

> **Leave** me be.
>
> **Let** me be.

Media, medium *Media* is plural. The singular is *medium*, but has nothing to do with size. Like *data* and *datum*, *phenomena* and *phenomenon*, one takes a plural verb and the other a singular verb.

Plural: Izzy Hahn thought that the **media** were responsible for the strained relationships between the Selectmen and the Police Department.

Singular: Charles Darecek and his wife Donna raved about the one **medium** that served the town best: The *Source* newspaper and **its** staff.

Nauseated, nauseous How language changes! In the 1960s, *nauseated* meant feeling sick, and **nauseous** meant disgusting or causing disgust. Now they are synonymous, according to *Webster's Collegiate*.

Nuclear *Nuclear* is on the list because of the pronunciation. Even famous people say "new-cue-ler." The proper pronunciation, of course, is "new-clee-er."

Or, nor *Or* goes with *either* and *nor* goes with *neither*. Like oil and water, they do not mix.

Either Muriel Scharf **or** her friend will volunteer to be hostess.

Monsignor Gerard Gaynor Schmitz **neither** runs a parish now **nor** does he care to; he now bosses other priests around.

Ordinance, ordnance An *ordinance* is a law set forth by a government, something ordained by fate or deity, or an order, usually from a recognized authority. *Ordnance* is artillery.

The Madison Town **ordinance** stating that only collies could be leashed and walked along Middle Beach Road caused heartache among several prominent residents who owned poodles.

If the six hundred horsemen knew of the **ordnance** facing them, they still marched on bravely. Ask Tennyson.

Orient (orientation), orientate If you *orient* a house, you build it to face easterly. If you *orient* a movie toward a particular audience, you write it differently than if you were writing for the general audience. If you acquaint students with rules and regulations, you are *orienting* classes to behaving properly. *Orientate* means to direct or face toward the east.

> **Wrong:** The principal exhorted his assistant to **orientate** the unruly sophomores.
>
> **Correct:** When praying, Muslims **orientate**.
>
> **Correct:** As soon as Captain Freytag got **oriented**, he drove the ship ever onward.

Palate, palette, pallet *Palate* means the roof of the mouth or taste, while *palette* is what the artist holds in one hand so that he can dab paint onto the brush. The mixture of paint is also a *palette*. A *pallet* is a small, hard, temporary bed or the portable rectangles of wood on which goods are stored in places like Costco, Sam's, and B.J.'s.

> Pepe's pizza on the first bite burns my **palate**.
>
> Phil Costello is the only cartoonist who holds a **palette** in his left hand as he rips into the locals and their foibles.

While Hughie Currie was transporting the **pallets** of house paint, he accidentally drove the tractor through the front window of Tuxis Lumber.

Peak, peek, pique Like the three preceding words, these three all sound alike, but there really should not be any confusion with them. *Peak* is the top, *peek* is the look, and *pique* is the irritating or arousing. *Pique* also is ribbed clothing of various materials or an inlaid tortoiseshell or ivory object.

Wendy Suzanne Podoloff **piqued** my interest in the Stones when I heard her singing during her workout session at Planet Fitness.

Angie Keyes reluctantly **peeked** into the cupboard after hearing some scurrying behind the door.

Todd Marshall Podolof told me that his golf game **peaked** when he shot a 71 at the New Haven Country Club.

Persecute, prosecute If one is *persecuted*, he is wronged somehow by torture, ridicule, or harassment. If one is *prosecuted*, he has the law brought against him.

If Alisha Nay "Peggy" Holmes ever felt **persecuted**, she would count to ten, eat an Oreo, and take a nap.

Once, Z Leach **prosecuted** the mail carrier because the latter frequently looked into certain packages delivered to Z's house.

Phenomenon, phenomena See **datum, data**.

PIN number Like *ATM*, *PIN* (as in PIN number) is redundant because the *N* means number.

Populace, populous *Populace*, a noun, refers to the residents of a town or city or institution, while *populous*, an adjective, means that an area has many people in it.

> Lois O'Neill Milligan thought that the **populace** of Clinton liked clams, the **populace** of Madison liked class, and the **populace** of Guilford adored culture.
>
> Linda Lee Milligan prefers **populous** areas centered around golf courses to crowded cities.

Precedence, precedents The first, *precedence*, implies priority of importance or the right to some high honor. The second, *precedents*, means that some things done or said serve as standards. People can be *precedents* also.

> Jack O'Connor, dressed as Uncle Sam, stomped up and down Middle Beach Road when the Boy Scouts were given **precedence** over him in Fourth of July Parade.
>
> Frank "Porky" Vieira set many **precedents** both in basketball at Quinnipiac and in baseball as coach of New Haven University.

Principal, principle I learned that the *principal* of a school is your "pal," an easy way to remember the spelling. If that statement is true, why do most students shake in their boots after being sent to his office? *Principals* in a movie or play are the main characters. *Principle* means a code of conduct or devotion to correctness.

> When Gilbert Cass was **principal** of Daniel Hand High School, he profoundly influenced the curricula in all subject areas.
>
> Paul Vincent Cochrane, a man of **principle**, would never think of sneaking into a movie theater while the usher was looking the other way.

Prioritize I first heard an assistant principal use this word when I first started teaching. I cringed then (1960) and I cringe now (2005). Perhaps, after I am pushing daisies, *prioritize* will be widely accepted; until then I believe that I am in the majority who think that this word is pretentious.

Queue, queueing What word other than *queueing* has five vowels in a row? A *queue*, especially in the UK, is a line. *Queueing* means that you are in line for something, possibly discount tickets in Leicester Square.

Quote, quotation Neither one of these words would be considered literary terms like *hyperbole* or *apostrophe*. A *quotation* is a passage referred to or the estimation of a bid on something. A *quote* is synonymous with *quotation*. Therefore to say: Macbeth seems heartless when, at the news of his wife's death he quotes, "She should have died hereafter," is incorrect because the author here is saying Macbeth quoted someone else.

> When I use the **quotation**, "Success is counted sweetest / By those who ne'er succeed" I am not referring to myself.

Reason, because See **because**.

Reoccurring A popular word among those who know not. The proper word is *recurring*.

Root, rout, route *Root* and *route* are sometimes pronounced the same. Sometimes *rout* and *route* are pronounced alike. *Router* is sometimes pronounced two different ways and then means two different things. *Root* sometimes rhymes with "boot" and sometimes rhymes with "foot." Who said English is easy?

Shall, will Many pages contain lengthy histories and explanations of these two words. *Shall* shows determination, simple futurity, or what is inevitable. *Will* indicates determination or persistence, frequent habitual action, and wishful intention. Are these two words interchangeable? Now? Perhaps. Years ago? No.

> A fan held up a sign during a game at the Meadowlands: "Thou **shall** not pass." (Sounds like some of my former teachers!)
>
> **Will** you stay the night?
>
> I **shall** pass the test with flying colors.
>
> I **will** mail the manuscript in the morning.
>
> I'**ll** be there for you.
>
> I'**ll** bet the family fortune on the horse named "Danny Boy."

Note: The last two example here are the reason, perhaps, that these words are becoming interchangeable.

So *So* should almost never be used by itself. *So* introduces clause with *that*.

> Jenny Lynn Scott was **so** taken by the city of Chicago **that** she decided to move there.
>
> Hollie Jean Flora-Holmquist decided to read *Grammar the Easy Way* **so that** she could write better letters.

Of course, the argument arises: *Webster's Collegiate* lists *so* as a pronoun:

> Sue Fusselman Ferrell felt that if she were to enroll in the French Foreign Legion, she should do **so** as soon as possible.

And as an adjective:

> Ann Merrifield Burham is beautiful by her own standards and **so** by others.

And as a conjunction:

> Lisa Greenwood Dapas did not want to read any of the literature extolling men, **so** she didn't.

I still hold that *so* should not be used by itself. Ever notice that when you say "So Big!" to babies and raise your arms, the babies raise their eyebrows? They instinctively know the usage of *so*.

Sort of, kind of Never use these in standard English to mean somewhat or rather. Sometimes using *rather*, however, you might give the impression, like the one Jordan Baker gave to Nick Carraway in *The Great Gatsby*, that you are balancing a glass on the end of your chin.

> Jan Za'jacka Hofmeister was **rather** (not *kind of* or *sort of*) shaken when presented with her hotel bill in Chicago.

Sort of a, kind of a In both cases, the *a* is redundant.

Split infinitives This problem has long been argued. I see nothing wrong, however, in saying that an infinitive, a verbal and a complete unit and a part of speech all in one, should not be split. If one can split an infinitive, why not split up other words that are considered whole: abso-freakin'-lutely—or marvel-lucious-ously.

> **Split:** Philip Roemer Dunne vowed **to never eat** in a restaurant that charged patrons for bread.

> **Correct:** Jane Thornbury Dunne also vowed **never to eat** in a restaurant that charged patrons for bread.

Note: You can lead a horse to water, you can rub your stomach and pat your head at the same time, and on a plane you can say "Hi, Jack" as long as your acquaintance is named "Jack," but you cannot split an infinitive.

Stationary, stationery Easiest way to remember the distinction between these two words is to remember *stationery* has an *er* just like *letter*, which is written on stationery. Or, if you are at the station waiting for the Blue Line El in Chicago, you are standing, that is, *stationary*.

That, which, who, whom Mark Twain once (again) said that he held up to suspicion those persons who used *that* to refer to people. I agree. Use *who* or *whom* to refer to people and *which* and *that* to refer to anything else that is not a person.

> **Wrong:** The man **that** I met in the station said that I should give his regards to Theresa Lynch. (**Whom** is correct.)
>
> **Correct:** The man **whom** I saw with Kaitlin Lynch was her uncle Steve.
>
> **Correct:** Catharina Lynch, **who** in one semester had more A+'s than anyone else in her class, made high honors consistently.
>
> **Correct:** Two of Stephen Gerard Lynch's pet peeves, of **which** there are many, are older bartenders (Uncle Festers, he calls them) who forget both to put on the bar lights and to turn on the television sets on the bar lights.

There are those who treat pets as part of the family and do refer to a pig, a ferret, or a parrot, or even an anaconda with *who*:

> Teri James once exclaimed, "**Who** is better, Hootie (her parrot) or Keith (her husband)? (And she was talking to the parrot.)

I would not argue with Teri.

The fact that A redundant phrase. *The fact* can be omitted without changing the meaning.

Wrong: The fact that Duncan Craig is in Honors English and AP Social Studies means that he is an excellent student.

Correct: That his mother Karin also graced Daniel Hand as an excellent student is attributed to her father Charlie Gebauer.

There is, there are Said quickly and contracted, *"There's flies in my soup!"* sounds correct. If one can remember that *there* is not the subject of the sentence, there will be no error.

> Crew Richard Kirst shouted, "**There are** several <u>reasons</u> I like school."
>
> Amelia Jean Kirst might become a little excited when **there is** a wild <u>turkey</u> in her backyard.

This, that, these, those Turn on most sporting events and hear things like "those type of pitches" or "these kind of horses." These words are simple to use: *This* and *that* are singular and describe singular nouns; *these* and *those* are plural and describe a plural noun. The corrections:

> Jason Feihner Hine said that **those** <u>types</u> of pitches are hard to see.
>
> Abigail Meredith Hine bets only **those** <u>kinds</u> of horses that are brown.

Unbelievable This word should not be used to describe something prodigious or stupendous as in "Inger Marie Mattern wrote the most unbelievable poem about piloting in San Francisco Bay." Strictly speaking, the word means not likely to be believed, so that to say the poem was unbelievable means it contained something preposterous.

Wrong: When Willie Mays had made that **unbelievable** catch from the bat of Vic Wertz in the Polo Grounds, he set a standard that no one will top. (Actually, if you look at the replay, it's close to being unbelievable.)

Correct: Leif Russell Mattern told an **unbelievable** story about a giant stalking the Whaler Vineyard in Ukiah, California.

Unique There are words, like *unique* that some "linguists" try to modify and make "more" **unique.** *Unique,* like *terrible, horrific,* and *huge,* stands alone and does not need qualifiers like the following: *most unique, very terrible, awfully horrific, big huge.*

Very Like the letter *c* by itself, here is a word one never needs to use. Why then, do most English teachers, myself included, use *very* to teach adverbs? *Very* easy. But *very* unique? *Very* terrible? *Very* horrific? *Very* nice? *Very* takes away from the words it describes. Sounds like the old Seinfeld series where a word is repeated several times within a few seconds: "Salsa, people like salsa; they like to say salsa; pass the salsa, I like salsa with noodles."

Vinegarette, vinaigrette Show me a restaurant that has *vinaigrette* spelled correctly (not *vinegarette*); then show me a restaurant where the staff pronounces *vinaigrette* with three syllables rather than four (veen-eh-gret vs. vin-eh-gar-ette). The Killingworth Inn is the only place I know that has it correct on the menu.

Way, ways Never use *ways* to mean distance. *Ways* is correct in the plural when synonymous with course, methods, or category. Use *way* to mean distance.

Weather, whether, wether All pronounced the same, these three words—the last one perhaps not widely used except on farms—are fairly easy to distinguish. The first is what one looks for on the TV and then is disappointed with the result; the second is usually used with *or not* or *no* or *or,* in situations that are questionable; the third is a castrated sheep or goat (doesn't the word look as if something is missing, too).

> Annie and Rusty Nyborg depend on the **weather** for a perfect crop of grapes for their Whaler Vineyard Red Zinfandel.

> Tara Leyne Nybord Larwood could not decide **whether** to send her parents to the Hand High Reunion (Class of '55) **or** to Disney World.

> **Whether or not** he would buy the old fire engine was never a concern for Danny Larwood.

Where, at Using these two words in the same sentence usually causes redundancy: **Where** is the phone **at**? A friend of mine once was accosted by a teenager with the following words: "Do you know **where** the library's **at**?" My friend said that yes, but where he came from, one never ends a sentence with a preposition. Whereupon the youngster came back with "Do you know **where** the library's **at**, you jerk."

Who, whom, whoever, whomever See Chapter Seven.

You, your, you're If you were born in Brooklyn, *youse* (as in *youse* guys) is what was heard. *You*, the second person singular or plural pronoun, unless in dialogue, should not be used in formal writing because it causes a shift in voice as in: "If <u>anglers</u> released more of the fish that they caught, **you**'d help conserve many species."

Your and *you're* pose another problem even though one should learn the distinction early on. *Your* is a possessive pronoun; *you're* is a contraction of *you are*. Not terribly difficult.

> Maria Grace Larwood said to her sister, Teak, "**You're** suggesting that we help Nana and Pop Pop harvest the grapes?"

> Reef Larwood said to her Uncle John Mattern once, "**Your** music sends me."

We introduce ourselves
To Planets and to Flowers
But with ourselves
Have etiquettes
Embarrassments
And awes

Emily Dickinson

Chapter Nine

SELECTING TOPICS TO WRITE ON . . .

If you are in school, topics for papers usually are given by the teachers. If you are not, then you must fend for yourself. I have always wondered where writers gathered ideas, and once, while I was reading an essay by Ernest Hemingway (in a collection of his newspaper stories) about *The Old Man and the Sea*, he told the reader that the idea for this novel came from a two-paragraph newspaper story about a Portuguese fisherman who was dragged about a hundred miles by a blue marlin.

The marlin and the fisherman reached shore—the man almost dead, the marlin a skeleton stripped by sharks. From that story came one of the great American novels.

In Chapter Ten, you will see the various topics used by poets—the list seems endless—until you start to write, that is. But things to write about are always there. I once asked a standup comedian where her material came from, and she replied, "My family, of course!" Then she told me about her journal that is always with her.

I, myself, keep two journals—one handwritten and portable, the other on my computer. Most of the entries concern fishing because I write articles on angling for newspapers and magazines, but I also chart a log of gaffes made in the media.

Here are two entries about fishing in Key West. Both helped me write a newspaper article:

> At Schooner's in Key West there's this guy sitting at the bar with an iguana on his head.

and

> Tony took us fishing on his new boat *Scraps*.

This is what the first entry turned into the introduction:

A guy walks into Schooner's Wharf bar with an iguana on his head. The bartender says, "Wow! That's something! Where'd ya get it?"

The iguana replied, "In Key West—there's lots of them."

The second became the focus: Fishing in the Keys.

> *Scraps* aptly named Tony's fishing boat docked at the Navy Base in Key West. The hull, an old gutted Luhr's from the mid sixties, housed a diesel engine that itself was a conglomeration of a Cummings, Cat, Honda, and Volvo, the loudest in Southern Florida. The unfinished engine cover, a well-organized arranger of hooks, sinkers, leaders, barrel swivels, nail clippers, pieces of dried squid and herring, and a measurement tool to determine legal fish . . .

Journal entries do not need to be elaborate—sometimes a word will do. The other day, as I tutored a youngster in vocabulary, the word *obfuscate* appeared seemingly out of nowhere. It's the kind of word that Emily Dickinson said you should tip your hat to. Just now, as I look into the journal, the word stares back. Someday I'll *Write On! obfuscate*. I do not want to confuse anyone.

Keep a journal—the rest will come . . . .

Tell all the Truth but tell it slant —
Success in Circuit lies
Emily Dickinson

Chapter Ten

FIGURATIVE LANGUAGE IN POETRY
(AND PROSE)

Figurative language, the stuff of poetry, enhances one's writing like the stars shining through a cloudless night, decorating an otherwise ordinary evening. It makes both the reader and the writer think creatively, not that writing in and of itself is not creative, but writing does elevate with the use figurative language.

I remember well instructing my sophomore class curriculum at Hand High School in Madison, Connecticut, that included "The Tempest" and "Macbeth" by Shakespeare, *Of Mice and Men* by John Steinbeck, "Sohrab and Rustum" by Matthew Arnold, *Lord of the Flies* by William Golding, short stories by Shirley Jackson and Saki, and *The Bridge of San Luis Rey* by Thornton Wilder. Shakespeare and Steinbeck were standards; Matthew Arnold had existed on another planet, thirty-five years ago, in Paul Van K. Thompson's English class at Providence College; Saki and Jackson were fairly new.

"Sohrab and Rustum" by Matthew Arnold, a staple in the Hand High School curriculum for decades (now no longer taught), revived my interest in poetry learned at Providence College. With its enchanting metaphors ("I muse what this young fox may mean . . .") and extended similes (which stand by themselves as stories within a story) still beckon me to pore through the magical lines. I love especially the simile describing the first meeting, early on, between father (Rustum) and son (Sohrab), though neither is aware of his relationship with the other until the end of the poem:

> And Rustum came upon the sand, and cast
> His eyes toward the Tartar tents. And saw
> Sohrab come forth, and eyed him as he came
> As some rich woman, on a winter's morn
> Eyes through her silken curtains the poor drudge
> Who with numb blacken'd fingers makes her fire—

At cock-crow, on a starlit winter's morn,
When the frost flowers the whiten'd window-panes—
And wonders how she lives, and what the thoughts
Of that poor drudge may be; so Rustum eyed
The unknown adventurous youth, who from afar
Came seeking Rustum, and defying forth
All the valiant chiefs; long he perused
His spirited air, and wonder'd who he was.

The passage encompasses many themes in a few lines: The bitter cold, crisp morning; the class distinction between drudge and employer—the veteran warrior (Rustum) looking upon the tyro soldier; the concern of the rich woman wondering about the psyche of her maid, echoing Rustum's concern for the youth he is about to battle; the alliteration ("frost flowers," "cock-crow," and "whiten'd-window-panes"); the transition from the simile to the main story of Sohrab and Rustum.

Matthew Arnold creates a miniepic with enough poetic convention to supply students and teachers with the essential language of poetry. Besides the great poetry, the narration itself tells an almost impossible and exciting story that is part of the culture of Iran.

As untragically as the poem ends (Sohrab does find his father whom he seeks but dies at the hands of his father, who, at the time of the fatal blow, does not realize he has killed his only son.), the beauty of the language along with metaphor, simile, alliteration (along with assonance and dissonance), hyperbole, onomatopoeia, personification, synecdoche (and metonymy), apostrophe, and iambic pentameter makes this piece of literature unforgettable.

Why not, then, consider beautifying a piece of prose with the above conventions. First, we'll let some of the famous ones help with examples of the above.

Metaphor: Metaphor is the direct comparison of two unlike things:

> The fog comes
> on little cat feet.
>
> It sits looking
> over harbor and city
> on silent haunches
> and then moves on.
>
> *"Fog" by Carl Sandburg*

An astounding metaphor written in prose? No, free verse, poetry that does not rhyme and has no meter—rhythm, yes—but no meter. With the simplest language, and only three simple verbs, the fog becomes a cat. Later on, Sandburg wrote a sonnet-like, free verse poem entitled "The Hangman at Home." Just the title evokes startling images, but the poem might be read if only for its creativity. (See Appendix Six for the complete poem.)

Then, with no verb, Emily Dickinson gives us

> A Route of Evanescence
> With a revolving Wheel . . .

and perfectly describes a hummingbird, and with

> I like to see it lap the Miles
> And lick the valleys up.

describes an "iron horse."

The point? Try describing in prose two unlike things—not in poetic form but in a paragraph. In a workshop given the English department at Hand High School in Madison, Connecticut, we were introduced to the computer, word processor to be exact, and we were instructed to create a prose piece of our choosing. I decided to have some fun and equate my first encounter with a computer and my first experience with sex—and I was called on to read it in front of the group, much to the delight of only two of my colleagues. After the reading, we were let go early—the metaphor too exciting.

Herman Melville wrote an essay, "I and My Chimney," where his chimney and Melville become a metaphor for a few pages. It starts:

> I and my chimney, two grey-headed old smokers, reside in the country [at Arrowhead in Pittsfield, Massachusetts]. We are, I may say, old settlers here; particularly my old chimney, which settles more and more every day.

In *Moby Dick* Melville writes a chapter, "The Monkey Rope." The entire essay is a metaphor comparing the rope tied around the waist of a man on deck (Ishmael) and connected to the man (Queequeg) just at the waterline, slicing into the whale. The idea, peculiar to the *Pequod*, was that the deckhand responsible for flensing was connected to the man on deck so that if anything

untoward befell the man flensing, both would probably drown or be eaten by sharks. In other words, it behooved the deckhand to be vigilant. The monkey rope, which connected the two men, becomes a metaphor for our connections to all sorts of people who live or die or benefit or suffer based on our actions. If I am caught stealing, for example, my entire family is connected to the shame.

Besides Melville, baseball, the only game according to Babe Ruth and some others, has contributed to the stockpile of metaphors:

Joe D. hit <u>frozen ropes</u>. (a screaming line drive)

Phil Rizzuto had three <u>Texas League singles</u> in one game. (bloop hits)

There's a <u>can o' corn.</u> (easy, catchable pop fly)

That ball was right in the batter's <u>wheelhouse.</u> (where his power lies)

Derek Jeter is a master of the <u>hook slide</u>. (a slide that resembles a hook because of the positioning of the leg touching the base)

A-Rod plays the <u>hot corner</u> now. (third base)

Mariano Rivera warms up in the <u>bullpen</u>. (usually an enclosed area for relief pitchers)

Joe Page of the Yankees was called "The <u>Fireman</u>." (he threw "heat")

Nolan Ryan threw <u>bullets</u>. (unseen fast balls)

Lou Aceto was called to <u>sacrifice</u>. (give up your turn at bat so that another runner may advance)

Fred Geier could throw that <u>pill</u>. (his fast ball looked small)

From the stands: "Hum that <u>pea</u>!" (referring to the apparent size of the ball)

Bob Feller threw <u>aspirin tablets</u>. (again referring to the size of the fast ball)

Simile: A simile is indirect comparison of two unlike things using the words *as*, *like*, or sometimes *than*.

Robert Frost wrote in "Birches":

> You may see their trunks arching in the woods
> Years afterwards, trailing their leaves on the ground
> Like girls on hands and knees that throw their hair
> Before them over their heads to dry in the sun.

And again in "Mending Wall," a narrative poem about a neighbor repairing winter damage to the stone wall separating two properties:

> I see him there
> Bringing a stone grasped firmly by the top
> In each hand, like an old-stone savage armed.

The image, a man "palming" two stones, looks more like a warrior in battle than a person fixing a fence. Incidentally, this poem is often misinterpreted because of the line "Good fences make good neighbors." That line came from the neighbor, not the narrator (Frost). Frost says, "Good fences do not make good neighbors."

And one more time for Matthew Arnold: Just after Rustum has delivered the fatal blow to his still unknown son (later on Rustum discovers the truth):

> And he saw that Youth
> Of age and looks to be his own dear son,
> Piteous and lovely, lying on the sand,
> Like some rich hyacinth which by the scythe

Of an unskilled gardener has been cut,
Mowing the garden grass-plots near its bed,
And lies, a fragrant flower of purple bloom,
On the mown, dying grass—so Sohrab lay,
Lovely in death, upon the common sand.

We see the "scythe" (the sword), the "some rich hyacinth" (From Rustum's eyes, Sohrab is just another one of his conquests, not the beautiful looking young warrior in his prime), and "purple" (suggesting the flower itself and a hint of the blood pouring from Sohrab).

Now, taking a cue from Shakespeare, I believe we need some comic relief with some sayings we learned as children:

Your teeth are like stars: They come out at night.
Your eyes are like the flag: red, white, and blue.
Your ears are like flowers: cauliflowers.

And baseball contributes here too:

He swings like a rusty gate.
It looked as if the pitcher pulled the string (when he threw a change-up).
The ball looked like a snow cone in his glove (but the catch was made, although the white of the ball showed at the top of the glove).

Try writing a paragraph or two using similes to make your point.

Alliteration: Alliteration is successive consonant sounds, usually two or more, at the beginning of words (*Fowler's* states that the sounds can come from the middle of the words too, but I was taught that was **dissonance.** I'm sure he is correct.) With certain letters, then, the poet achieves the added dimension of sound that helps enhance the reader's experience.

Classic Shakespeare I will start with.

> Tomorrow, and tomorrow, and tomorrow
> Creeps in this petty pace from day to day . . .

Then let's move up a few centuries to Poe:

> Helen, thy beauty is to me
>   Like those Nicean barks of yore,
> That gently, o'er a perfumed sea,
>   The weary, way-worn wanderer bore . . .

And finally look at the first line of stanza three of "The Raven":

> And the silken, sad, uncertain rustling of each purple
> curtain . . .

Assonance: Assonance occurs with vowel sounds that are exact or close. *Pike* and *strike* are an example of true rhyme, while *pike* and *strife* are an example of assonance or off-rhyme because the consonants following the rhyming vowels are different. Was Emily Dickinson playing with our ears when she wrote

> At Half past Three, a single Bird
> Unto a silent sky
> Propounded but a single term
> Of cautious melody.

> *and*

This World is not conclusion
A Species stands beyond—
Invisible, as Music—
But positive, as Sound—

Hyperbole: Hyperbole is exaggeration for effect. Consider the clichéd hyperbole: "I've told you a million times to clean your room!" The rude answer to that statement might be, "Mom, a million times? You'd still be talking!"

Matthew Arnold has a better example from "Sohrab and Rustum":

But Sohrab heard, and quail'd not, but rush'd on,
And struck again; and again Rustum bow'd
His head; but this time all the blade, like glass,
Sprang in a thousand shivers on the helm . . .

And from Ralph Waldo Emerson:

Here once the embattled farmers stood.
And fired the shot heard round the world.

Again, with that second line above, baseball comes to mind, when, in 1951, Bobby Thomson, against Ralph Branca, hit the "shot heard round the world" as The New York Giants beat the Dodgers for the National League pennant. And for you trivia fans, who was the man on deck? Willie Mays, of course.

Onomatopoeia: Just the spelling of onomatopoeia is a challenge; it is the sound of the word reflecting its meaning. What immediately comes to mind is the Batman comic books where on every page the dynamic duo were dispatching the members of the evil empires with a "POW" or "BIFF" or "SLAM," those words indicating the name of the sound.

Emily Dickinson: I heard a fly <u>buzz</u> when I died . . .

Lord Tennyson: The <u>moan</u> of doves in immemorial elms
And <u>murmuring</u> of innumerable bees . . .

Edgar Alan Poe: Bells, bells, bells, bells, bells, bells . . .

Major League baseball: The <u>crack</u> of the bat (in college and high school, the <u>ping</u> of the bat)

Personification: Personification allows the writer to give human characteristics to those items that are not human:

Emily Dickinson: Because I could not stop for Death—
He kindly stopped for me . . .

and

A word is dead,
When it is said,
Some say.

I say it just begins
To live that day.

Sylvia Plath ("Mirror" speaks):

I am silver and exact
I have no preconceptions
Whatever I see I swallow immediately
Just as it is, unmisted by love or dislike.
I am not cruel, only truthful.

Synecdoche (and Metonymy): Two of the most difficult poetic terms to define, both synecdoche and metonymy are specific forms of metaphor. Broadly speaking, synecdoche is a part of something to represent the entity, and metonymy is one entity, closely related but not a part or piece of, standing for another. Now let us be more specific.

Synecdoche is a part of something representing the whole. In the following sentences, the examples of synecdoche are underlined:

A. "Nice <u>threads</u>," my friend Ben Lockhart said admiring my new Brooks Brothers camel hair overcoat.

B. Ronald E. Catania would rather fish from a <u>head</u> boat than from a charter.

C. Dana Valieray produced a <u>set of wheels</u> admired by all the bikers in the area: his souped-up, $45,000 version of a 1979 Harley. (Check out "bikers"; it's an example of metonymy.)

The material something is made with stands for that item:

A. "Can I put my taxes on <u>plastic</u>," I asked Alma the tax collector as I handed her my American Express card.

B. As Joe Gugliclmo strode toward the plate with a thirty-four inch <u>ash</u>, he eyed the distant left field fence and the sign that said, "Air pockets are the worst."

Sometimes synecdoche occurs when the species is substituted for the genus:

A. The <u>suicide bomber</u> failed in his attempt to assassinate the mayor of the town.

B. If the pen is mightier than <u>steel</u>, when I prick myself with my <u>Mt. Blanc</u>, do I lose a finger?

Metonymy is the reference to person or things by naming one of their attributes or something closely associated with them.

    A. Reading <u>Edith Wharton</u> takes concentration.

    B. Rod Bascomb is definitely a <u>Mercedes</u> when it comes to driving.

    C. John Conti, a devout man of the <u>cloth</u>, graduated from Notre Dame High School, West Haven, Connecticut, in 1955.

    D. <u>Fins and Feathers</u>, a redundant magazine, gave me an opportunity to start my writing career.

    E. Word came from the <u>Oval Office</u> that terrorist activities were expected to increase in the next two years.

Apostrophe: Apostrophe is the language device used by authors to speak to someone or something whether that person or thing is present or not. Henry Fielding quite frequently addressed the reader in *Tom Jones*; poets spoke to Erato, the Muse of poetry, for inspiration; Ralph Waldo Emerson communicated with a flower and a bee, probably in front of a fire in some cozy den:

Flower: Rhodora! if the sages ask thee why
           This charm is wasted on earth and sky,
           Tell them, dear, that if eyes were made for seeing,
           Then Beauty is its own excuse for being.

                                  "The Rhodora"

Bee: burly, dozing, humble-bee,
           Where thou art is clime for me.

                                 "The Humble-Bee"

And Walt Whitman spoke to many:

> O powerful western fallen star!
> O shades of night—O moody, tearful night!

> O cruel hands that hold me powerless . . .
> "When Lilacs Last in the Dooryard Bloom'd"

Iambic Pentameter: This poetic form, used by Shakespeare for those important parts in his plays (ruffians and lowlifes spoke mostly in prose) and in his sonnets, designates a line of poetry that contain five (*penta*) iambs, which are poetic feet of two syllables, the first unstressed and the second stressed. Somewhere I read that Shakespeare wrote the thirty-seven plays in mostly iambic pentameter because he said that we tend to talk that way anyway, that is if you are not French. The last statement sounds as if Mark Twain said it.

E. A. Robinson (whom you do not want to read if you are depressed) wrote the majority of his poetry in this form:

> Cliff Klingenhagen had me in to dine
> With him one day; and after soup and meat,
> And all the other things we had to eat,
> Cliff took two glasses and filled one with wine
> And one with wormwood. Then, without a sign
> For me to choose at all, he took the draught
> Of bitterness himself, and lightly quaffed
> It off, and said the other one was mine.

Read the first stanza of "Richard Cory" by E. A. Robinson:

> Whenever Richard Cory went downtown,
> We people on the pavement looked at him.
> He was a gentleman from sole to crown,
> Clean-favored and imperially slim.

The poem reads with hidden, but obvious, rhythm; each line is exactly ten syllables, five iambs, in other words, iambic pentameter. Test it. Notice that the first syllable in each iamb is unaccented and the second is accented. However, if you read this poem out loud, you notice not so much the rhythm, although it's there, but that you are speaking normally. There are other forms of meter, but iambic pentameter historically was used in the beginning of poetry (*Beowulf, Iliad, Odyssey, Aenied, Paradise Lost*).

These examples of figurative language, not limited to poetry, enable writers to delight the senses all ways. I can think of many writers, famous for prose, who also wrote beautiful poetry: Emerson, Hawthorne, Melville, Poe, to name a few. Try your hand at writing figurative language.

THE SUBJECTS OF POETRY

I often think of a poem by Gerry Degenhardt, my colleague for several years. He had taken a trip to Florida, took a wrong turn while there, and drove past a hovel with a wedding dress for sale displayed on the front patch of lawn. He wrote

> For Sale
> When it is car or boat
> Or even some sweet remnants
> Of a house —
> Anyone may understand
> Why an owner
> Might wish to rid himself
> Of these
> And take the time
> To paint a sign

FOR SALE

But I must admit
I was moved
Beyond all other signs
That sit and stare
On lawns at passing cars
Inviting stops
For "anywhoknowswhats"
To come inside
To loll and gossip
To touch and maybe buy a past
That's used
And very likely gone –

When I drove 44 East
Cassia, Florida
As poor as it is flat
Saw a painted wooden sign
Among some palms
And oaks of dripping moss

FOR SALE HERE

WEDDING

GOWN

Used with permission of the author

Looking for something to write about? Look to the poets for topics:

- Make light of those who go to church once a week:

  > Some keep the Sabbath
  > Going to Church—
  > I keep it staying at Home . . . .

  Emily Dickinson

- Find a unique way of judging a person:

  > Men of the woods and lumberjacks,
  > They judged me by their appropriate tool.
  > Except as a fellow handled an ax
  > They had no way of knowing a fool.

  Robert Frost

- Edgar Lee Masters wrote about people speaking from the grave:

  > Tom Merritt
  > At First I suspected something—
  > She acted so calm and absent-minded.
  > And one day I heard the back door shut,
  > As I entered the front, and saw him slink
  > Back of the smokehouse into the lot,
  > And run across the field.
  > But that day, walking near Fourth Bridge,
  > Without a stick or a stone at hand,
  > All of a sudden I saw him standing,
  > Scared to death, holding his rabbits,
  > And all I could say was, "Don't, Don't, Don't,"
  > As he aimed and fired at my heart.

  From the Spoon River Anthology

- What was like for a hangman to come home to his family after he put in a day of hard work? See Appendix Six for Carl Sandburg's "Hangman at Home."
- In Robert Frost's "Out, Out—, a young man is cutting wood with a buzz saw and accidentally cuts his hand off. The title of the poem comes from *Macbeth*, Act V, "Out, out, brief candle . . . ." Macbeth here is referring to life that is meaningless, but Frost is telling the story of the death of a youngster working a man's job.
- Longfellow wrote a poem entitled "Jewish Cemetery in Newport." You can visit the exact place in Newport, Rhode Island, and perhaps be inspired to write on many different topics there—especially sailing. Do not be surprised to see the gravestones there with Portuguese names.
- When he was a teenager, William Cullen Bryant wrote "Thanatopsis," a poem about death. Bryant's father, the story goes, found the poem in a drawer, sent it to Richard Henry Dana, and Dana thought that the father, not the son, had written it.
- John Greenleaf Whittier wrote a poem of couplets about a ninety-year-old woman who, while defending the flag of our country, stood up to Stonewall Jackson:

  > "Shoot if you must, this old gray head,
  > But spare your country's flag," she said.

- Edgar Allan Poe composed a poem about a raven that could say, "nevermore."
- Walt Whitman, considered one of the greatest American poets, once wrote an essay about why he hated school. Of course, he is most remembered for "Leaves of Grass," which

shows his power of observation. He was also a nurse during the Civil War.

- In her poem "Observation," Dorothy Parker says if she does certain things, her life would get better. The last two lines let us know her decision for the future:

> But I shall stay the way I am,
> Because I do not give a damn.

- T. S. Eliot wrote about cats, and that poem became "Cats," the Broadway musical.
- Marianne Moore wrote an ode to a snail.
- Clam diggers are aided in their quest for quahogs by Wilbert Snow's "Advice to a clam-digger."
- In a statement about an observation, Vachel Lindsay entitled one of her poems, "Factory Windows Are Always Broken."
- Claude McKay, who was born in Jamaica and later moved to New York City, wrote about "The Subway Wind," which straphangers know all too well.
- Archibald MacLeish, who graduated Yale Phi Beta Kappa, on poetry:

> A poem should not mean
> But be

- Irving Berlin's "Slumming on Park Avenue" speaks for itself.
- Cole Porter on modern authors:

> Good authors too who once knew better words
> Now only use four-letter words
> Writing prose,
> Anything goes.

- Eamon Grennan wrote a poem called "The Bat." In it he describes being in a room where a bat has flown and is trying to get out. Like Frost, he transforms an experience of nature into an experience of life.

- There are two ways of experiencing Maya Angelou's poetry: Listen to her recite or read them yourself. Listening to her is an experience everyone should enjoy.

- Bonnie (Murphy) Leigh, one of my former students from the 1960s, writes many of her own songs and revised this one especially for me. It's called "These Old Eyes," and is printed with Bonnie's permission:

> Just yesterday, my Dad and I
> Went out to lunch to pass the time
> At Lynch & Malone's near Murphy's General Store
> He talked of how the world had changed
> From his youth to what now remained
> A mystery to what we're headed for
>
> What these old eyes have seen, my father told me
> What these old eyes have seen
>
> A memory of days before
> When people didn't lock their door
> And strangers found a safe place in the night
> Now cities built where wildlife roam
> And children run away from home
> The sky's so brown, you can not see the light

What these old eyes have seen, what these old eyes
have seen

    Does the thought occur to those so young
    With jewelry mounted on their tongue
    The future lies within their generation

    So much unrest throughout the world
    A little boy, or a little girl
    Will grow up to lead this great nation

A longing for serenity
A place to live that's wild and free
Where neighbors say "Hello!" to one another
The computer age is growing fast
A youngster's childhood doesn't last
When will we come to love one another?

What these old eyes have seen, what these old eyes
have seen

We finished coffee and stood to leave
He turned around and looked at me
And said, "Bonnie, don't you worry over much.
Have faith in our humanity
And just thank God for sanity
And folks like you and me are still in touch."

What these old eyes have seen, he reassured me
What these old eyes have seen
What these old eyes have seen, my father told me
What these old eyes have seen!

The subjects of poetry, then, seem vast; why cannot the subjects of prose, therefore, be just as vast? "I can't think of anything to write" stands next to "I don't like the topic you gave me" in the book of English teachers' frustrations so that some educators, possibly out of frustration, called for "brainstorming" sessions. I never really knew what that term meant; my solution was to have the students turn on the TV for five minutes, jot down some topics presented, and write about one of them. Or, the students could take a newspaper or magazine, flip through the pages until something caught their attention, and write about that topic. In a sense I was asking them to "brainstorm," but I disliked the term then— and now.

Perhaps the best idea is to have a pen and notebook handy at all times, and when some interesting tidbit arises, the writer is ready to *Write On!*

Babble of the Happy
Cavil of the bold

Emily Dickinson

Chapter Eleven

LEVELS OF LANGUAGE

"Should I ask for the money in iambic pentameter?"

Formal standard English, informal standard English, and the generally unacceptable English, the three recognized levels of language most writers ascribe to, have entertained, informed, educated, persuaded, and aided readers since the beginning of time. Even Shakespeare and the Elizabethan theatergoer appreciated two of the levels when The Bard had most noble, and some ignoble, characters speak in iambic pentameter, while thugs and hooligans spoke in prose without the meter but with all the decorations of figurative language. In *Macbeth*, for example, after Macduff playfully asks the drunken porter:

> M: What three things does drink especially provoke?

The porter answers with the following, in prose, not iambic pentameter:

> DP: Marry, sir, nose-painting, sleep, and urine. Lechery, sir, it provokes and unprovokes: it provokes the desire but it takes away the performance. Therefore much drink may be said to be an equivocator with lechery: it sets him on and it takes him off; it persuades him and disheartens him, makes him stand to and not stand to; in conclusion, equivocates him in a sleep, and giving him the lie, leaves him.

The speech is lewd, suggestive, filled with puns, and typical of the speeches Elizabethans loved. And most of them stood to watch—The Globe Theater in London was their playground.

On our playground and away from parents, we learned the generally unacceptable language, the kind one doesn't use in front of Aunt Martha, and we found out that if adults heard this language, punishment would follow. "Vulgar" terms just were never appropriate.

Later on, when we became streetwise, language took on an identity that many adults scoffed at but sometimes used themselves. The sound of "phat," "the bomb," "rad," "boss," "rents," and "dis" became common. Curses were prevalent too, but the argot of teenage years abounded with esoteric, mostly monosyllabic utterances.

Our knowledge of informal language grew faster than that of our formal standard English, but as we progressed through college, professors hammered away at the proper use of words like *imply* and *infer*, *less* and *fewer*, and *number* and *amount*. (See Chapters Seven and Eight.) Gradually, the three levels of language became clear, and then it was time to teach our children and grandchildren what we had learned. Of course, the special words they used were as unintelligible to us as ours were to our parents.

FORMAL STANDARD ENGLISH

Formal standard English one can use in all situations, even though sometimes on the street we see some scratching of heads. This type of language must dominate a letter to the editor, a college essay, a term paper, historical and scientific research, and op-ed pieces: There is very little room for other levels of language.

Sir Francis Bacon writes

> The human understanding is of its own nature prone to abstractions and gives a substance and reality to things which are fleeting. But to resolve nature and abstractions is less to our purpose than to dissect her into parts; as did the school of Democritus, which went further into nature than the rest. Matter rather than forms should be the object of our atten-

tion, its configurations and changes of configuration, and simple action, and law of action or motion; for forms are figments of the human mind, unless you will call those laws of action forms.

From "Novuum Organum"
(loosely translated into "imaginative")

Or consider this selection from the autobiography of John Stuart Mill:

For some years after this time [1828] I wrote very little, and nothing regularly, for publication.: and great were the advantages which I derived from the intermission. It was of no common importance to me, at this period, to be able to digest and mature my thoughts for my own mind only, without any immediate call for giving them out in print. Had I gone on writing, it would have much disturbed the important transformation in my opinions and character, which took place during those years. The origin of this transformation, or at least the process by which I was prepared for it, can only be explained by turning some distance back.

INFORMAL ENGLISH

Formal standard English, then, is appropriate for every occasion. Informal language, on the other hand, has its own niche. In the words of John Stuart Mill: Poetry, when it is really such, is truth; and fiction, also, if it is good for anything, is truth . . . . Paul Lawrence Dunbar wrote such real poetry in "When Malindy Sings."

G'way an' quit dat noise, Miss Lucy—
Put dat music book away;
What's de use to keep on tryin'?
Ef you practise twell you're gray,
You cain't sta't no notes a flyin'
Lak de ones dat rants and rings
F'om de kitchen to de big woods
When Malindy sings.

As did Mark Twain in *Huckleberry Finn* write "reality" fiction as Jim says

". . . What you want to know when good luck's a-comin' for? want to keep it off?" . . . "Ef you's got hairy arms en a hairy bres', it's a sign dat you's agwyne to be rich. Well, dey's some use in a sign like dat, 'kase it's so fur ahead. You see, maybe you's got to be po' a long time fust, en so you might git discourage' en kill yo'sef 'f you did n' know by de sign dat you gwyne to be rich bymeby."

UNACCEPTABLE ENGLISH

Inappropriate language, scorned by a few and used by many, is known by many terms such as *earthy*, *salty*, *coarse*, *gross*, *lewd*, *Pete's way*, or even *common*. *Webster's Eleventh Collegiate* defines a vulgarism as "a word or expression originated or used chiefly by illiterate persons." Having used vulgarities, should a person be looked down upon? Perhaps in gray areas we need to be thinking, "There is nothing good or bad but thinking makes it so." One fact remains clear: Sometimes speakers are judged by the language they use.

"Classic": A book which people praise and don't read.
Mark Twain

Chapter Twelve

A READING LIST TO MAKE BETTER WRITERS

Student to teacher: Shakespeare talks funny.

If Ernest Hemingway was correct, a good writer needs to be a good reader—of dead writers. He thought that writers living were still learning their craft and are of note, but the dead ones remain famous forever. Hemingway caught Marlin with the experts, he led an exciting, if sometimes questionable, life, and he wrote mainly about his experiences. *The Old Man and the Sea* he based on two paragraphs from a newspaper about a Portuguese fisherman who was dragged out to sea by a huge marlin. The short story "The Short Happy Life of Francis MacComber" is also partially autobiographical.

Hemingway's topics, limited, perhaps, because his writing may have been interrupted by a tryst or two, exemplify what Daniel Francis Xavier Mulvey, Sports Editor of the *New Haven Register*, used to say about writing: "Write about what you know." Hemingway knew about wars, about marlins, about all sorts of hunting, and about relationships with women.

Writers know things three ways: through experience (actually doing), through observation (things are happening to the writer), and by reading—dead writers, yes, but also great living writers. Reading opens doors to all sorts of ideas, and by example, I will turn again to my favorite novel, *Moby Dick* by Herman Melville. Reading this complicated novel takes patience—according to David Denby of *The New Yorker*, reading any fiction requires patience—but the rewards total infinity.

List of Topics Presented in *Moby Dick*

1. A study of whales (an entire chaper, "Cetolgy," is devoted to the various kinds of whales).

2. A remarkable description of different types of characters. From the sophisticated Aunt Charity to the

savage Queequeg, one can enter the minds of characters never to be met in person.

3. A powerful story line. Without question *Moby Dick* has a superb plot, although interrupted here and there with chapter-sized footnotes; the climax is without equal, powerful enough to remain etched in the careful reader's brain.

4. Classic situations of behavior. Queequeg, not knowing what a wheelbarrow was for, piled his things into it and hoisted the barrow, over his head, to his quarters—much to the delight of those watching him; Stubb insisting Fleece, the coal-black cook, deliver a stirring sermon to the sharks; Father Mapple in the chapel, climbing into the pulpit by way of a rope ladder, and then, before delivering his sermon on Jonah, pulling the rope ladder into the pulpit, symbolizing his withdrawal from mankind; Flask, the third mate, talking to the whale he is about to finish off; Ahab controlling the minds of the mates and the crew; Starbuck, the first mate, trying to persuade Ahab that what he, the captain, was about to do was wrong; Pip's lunacy revealing truths; Tashtego, the Gay Head Indian, nailing the flag to the mast of the sinking ship; Moby Dick, the white whale, seemingly human in his revenge; gams with the other whalers reporting of their sightings (or not) of the great white whale.

5. The processing of whales after their capture.

6. The realization that the *Pequod*, under the captaincy of Ahab, resembles the world because of the various nationalities from all over.

THE READING LIST TO MAKE BETTER WRITERS (IN NO CERTAIN ORDER OR GENRE)

All of Shakespeare, including the sonnets

Ethan Frome by Edith Wharton: Taught primarily in the eleventh grade, this novel contains excellent SAT vocabulary, a story that starts in the present, reflects to the past, and ends in the present.

The Scarlet Letter by Nathaniel Hawthorne: This classic, it seems, finds its way into almost every curriculum, especially in the junior year of high school. The setting is old Boston; one of the themes is very modern adultery, and the vocabulary is all Hawthorne, all SAT. *The Marble Faun* is both a novel and a travel guide to old Rome, while *The House of the Seven Gables*, set in Salem, Massachusetts, gives the reader a portrait of both a house and its environs. One can still visit the house in Salem and, while there, visit the Custom House where Hawthorne worked and wrote.

Huckleberry Finn, Tom Sawyer, Life on the Mississippi, and *Innocents Abroad* by Mark Twain all should be read by the time one reaches senior high school. Then, later on, they should be read again. I do not know how many times I have read *Huckleberry Finn*, but there are passages I can recite, and often do, to anyone who cares to listen. Also, *The Autobiography of Mark Twain*, published after his death for obvious reasons (he chastised Bret Harte, among others), is an ideal example of anyone attempting some sort of autobiography.

Henry James: Like William Cullen Bryant, Henry James first appeared in the *Atlantic Monthly* and then went on to write *Portrait of a Lady, The Ambassadors, The Wings of a Dove,* and *The Golden Bowl.* Sometimes avoided by high school, James nevertheless is must reading for future writers.

The Jungle by Upton Sinclair: This novel created a stir in, and revolutionized, the meatpacking business. There are scenes in this novel so graphic that it takes a strong stomach to get through without retching.

Of Mice and Men (East of Eden, Grapes of Wrath, The Pearl) by John Steinbeck: *Of Mice and Men,* originally started as a drama for stage but turned into a novel first because his dog ate the script, prompted Steinbeck to praise his dog as an astute critic. Steinbeck does not use much SAT vocabulary here, but students really take to this novel fast.

Short stories ("The Cask of Amontillado" and so on) of Edgar Allan Poe: "William Wilson," read carefully, explores the mind of Poe and his powerful vocabulary.

All the novels and short stories of Thomas Hardy (*The Mayor of Casterbridge, Return of the Native, Far from the Madding Crowd,* and so on): Hardy, like Dickens, gives the reader an idea of what England was like years ago: Hardy depicted the rural aspect of England, while Dickens portrayed mostly the city.

Catcher in the Rye by J. D. Salinger: As Holden Caufield sits with his psychiatrist and asks him if he really wants to hear the story, J. D. Salinger draws the reader into *Catcher in the Rye,* a book that began its journey in the college curricula and worked its way down to the junior high level.

Anything by Pat Conroy: Pat Conroy's books contain interesting stories based on obvious truth. From the corruption at a military academy to the saving of sea turtles from destruction, Conroy uses SAT vocabulary better than most.

All the novels by John Irving: John Irving became recognized with Garp (and *Cider House Rules, Hotel New Hampshire, Son of the Circus*), furthered with Owen Meany, and in 2005 released another magical, often bizarre, and heavily criticized novel of a journey, beginning in Scandinavia, *Until I Find You*. One can expect Irving's writing to be perfectly outrageous, worthy of a college English professor.

The Great Gatsby by F. Scott Fitzgerald: *The Great Gatsby*, sometimes called "The Great American Novel" because an era is captured within a story of someone trying to bring back the past, has plenty of SAT vocabulary. A close reading is essential. *Tender Is the Night* is worth reading also, as are many of his short stories.

Catch-22, by Joseph Heller: This book "should be read out loud" according to my high school English teacher, Chuck Collins. While you are at it, try "The Crucible."

An American Tragedy, Sister Carrie, Jennie Gerhardt, "The Financier," "The Titan," and "The Stoic" by Theodore Dreiser: Women do not fare well in many of his stories, and some men appear ruthless in their domination of their environment. One learns many things about growing up in America during the early part of the twentieth century.

Native Son and *Blackboy* by Richard Wright: These two books, not to mention several of his short stories ("The Man Who Knew Too Much"), especially the "newer, unexpurgated" versions, are must readings. When the Book of the Month Club selected both novels as its selections of the month, Wright was asked to leave out some parts that seemed, at the time, too controversial for the general reading audience. I wonder if he would do that today?

Lord of the Flies by William Golding: A standard in most high school curricula, this book makes for interesting discussion.

Sherwood Anderson: If you're going to read anything by Sherwood Anderson, it might be *Winesburg, Ohio*.

Lolita by Vladimir Nabokov: *Lolita* is controversy at its best, the writing craft at its best; it is a study of not only perversion but also writing brilliance. The vocabulary demands a dictionary at hand.

The French Lieutenant's Woman by John Fowles: I have read this book three times because of the spellbinding pattern of words. I think that if I were Benjamin Franklin, I would imitate the writing in this novel above all others.

Lord Jim, The Heart of Darkness, and the short story "Youth" by Joseph Conrad: Conrad's works show how narrative can be long, drawn out, and still riveting.

Invisible Man by Ralph Ellison: This novel, on hundreds of reading lists, is essential reading for the beginning writer.

Ironweed and any other novel by William Kennedy (also an English professor): Kennedy captures life in and around Albany, New York. The characterization ranks with the best.

As I Lay Dying, Light in August, and *The Sound and the Fury* by William Faulkner: All are must reads.

Works by Sinclair Lewis: Lewis' novels used to be on many reading lists, but they still should be read—especially *Main Street, Babbitt, Arrowsmith, Cass Timberlane,* and *Elmer Gantry.*

The Souls of Black Folk by W. E. B. Du Bois, who grew up in Great Barrington, Massachusetts, is most interesting.

Poets recommended (in no order): Edgar Allan Poe, William Cullen Bryant, Edwin Arlington Robinson, Robert Frost, Emily Dickinson, Walt Whitman, Henry David Thoreau (and *Walden Pond*), Ralph Waldo Emerson (and all of his essays), Eamon Grennan, Carl Sandburg (and his work on Abraham Lincoln), Henry Wadsworth Longfellow, John Greenleaf Whittier, Paul Lawrence Dunbar, Langston Hughes, Claude McKay, Maya Angelou, James Weldon Johnson, Arna Bontemps, Countee Cullen, and Gerald Degenhardt.

This is the start of a reading list. Obviously, it reflects a personal view and has left out many worthwhile challenges. Thomas Wolfe once worried that he would pass on before he could read all the important books of the world, but if you read *Look Homeward, Angel,* you will find an extensive reading list to begin your quest. Above all, remember the premise: Good readers make good writers.

*The test of a man or woman's breeding is
how they behave in a quarrel.*

George Bernard Shaw

Chapter Fourteen

THE TEST
(OF YOUR WRITING BREEDING)

Student to teacher: If I do not dot
the "i's" will you take points off?

Like many hotels that don't have a thirteenth floor, this book does not really contain a "thirteenth" chapter; besides, taking a test on a book might be unlucky anyhow, especially if the test taker does not do well. Here are fifty sentences or groups of sentences. Some are correct. Some have one error, some two (but no more than two). If you score 80 percent or better, you might need a little coaching—but not much. Anything below that, you need some honing. In any case, good luck; if you are curious, the answers follow after item 50. Word of advice: Do not do these in order, but rather choose the ones you identify first.

1. Wriggling back and forth, Paul Michael Randall had a difficult time catching the snake.

2. Brian Mark Randall told his brother that he was going to meet Magic Johnson.

3. Donna Mae Holcombe Randall tried sailing on Bantam Lake, dabbled in the leather craft, and running for First Selectman of Morris, Connecticut.

4. Dennis Alfred "The Great" Randall planted several begonias along the lakefront at Bantam and was asked to join the Garden Club of Western Connecticut.

5. Because David Allen Randall rooted for the Red Sox, he did not allow anyone in his family to mention the Yankees.

6. When Steven Dennis Randall entered his first year in school, he was only able to take one reading course.

7. Preciosa de Jesus Alves Baltazar Krause, along with her husband and two friends, go to Europe in the spring.

8. Peter Edwin Krause a retired English teacher and world traveler loves to play golf during the rain.

9. Martha Helen Garbo loves to tell Irish jokes, and sometimes she forgets the punch lines.

10. John Robert Garbo traveled to Florida as a teenager, writes poetry while en route, and generally cause excitement everywhere he went.

11. Roberta Lynn Lockhart, a pediatrician with a practice in Milford, Connecticut, is extremely interested in the curriculum at Hopkins.

12. Beside Ron Harris Freytag, Joe Farnsworth Gallagher was chosen as Bartender of the Year in a New England popularity contest.

13. As Susan Louise Freytag walked in the room, all eyes riveted on her.

14. If only Dean Harold Zanardi when he paved the Mulvey's driveway in the middle of a heat wave in July.

15. Denise Aurora Zanardi wrote poetry like no other, sang spirituals to no one in particular, and danced her way into the hearts of her neighbors, which made her the most popular lady on the block.

16. When Brett David Zanardi and Paul Daniel Zanardi spoke, people listened.

17. With too many plates and cups to carry into the dining room, Lindsey Ann Johnson couldn't find one to carry them with.

18. Joe Frank Bruno found an old bat in his attic that he used to swing when he was younger.

19. Because she adapted the kitten left on her doorstep, Lisa Ann Kasersky was voted Humanitarian of the Year.

20. If Bill Lyman Cotter had chosen another profession he might not have had as much success as he did.

21. Not only did Courtney Fellows Cotter reap rewards for selling the most houses for her company she donated a serious lump of money also to the Louisiana Relief effort.

22. When Don Gates interviewed Tom Purcell for the job of Superintendent of Schools, he had no idea of his arrest the previous year.

23. Kippy Vioretta Martin or some of her friends from the Bronx is responsible for giving that area of New York a good name.

24. Gabrielle Whitney Martin loves to read any book put in front of her, delights in cartoon shows that feature animals, and relishes the first day of school as if it were going to heaven.

25. When Gregory Wayne Martin II saved an old lady from drowning, rescued a kitten from behind a neighbor's chimney, and jumped into a runaway car and brought it to a complete stop just before it might have entered a crowded playground—all in one day—he did not think it was anything to cheer about.

26. As Kyle Vincent Martin was exiting the school bus in front of her house, her best friend and neighbor said that she would meet her in about an hour.

27. Whatever caused Kyla Vioretta Martin to scream during the night remains a mystery to her mother and father.

28. Angelina Rita Syme did not know whether to attend a lecture on retirement or should she stay home and vacuum the cellar.

29. The reason Eric and Peter Weiss moved in together was because it would mean they could share the exorbitant taxes in their new adopted town.

30. When Robert Paul Yonkey casted his custom-made lure toward the jumping snappers, the line broke, the sinker crashed through a nearby window, and he smirked like he was saying, "I meant to do that."

31. Summer bombarded the Nantucket residents with unbearable heat while spring, waiting for next year, gloated about her performance just a few months before, and Sally Ann Ward moved off the island.

32. Paul Douglas "Brokaw" Hinman holds court almost every morning at the Circle Luncheonette he often talks politics, mentions "Roadkill," and in general entertains anyone who wishes to listen.

33. Either Ryan A. Duques or James Warner, both editors of several newspapers in Connecticut, prove that despite their English teacher one can succeed with words.

34. Cannery Row in Monterey in California is a poem, a stink, a grating noise, a quality of light, a tone, a habit, a nostalgia, a dream.

35. Cannery Row is the gathered and scattered, tin and iron and rust and splintered wood, chipped pavement and weedy lots and junk heaps, sardine canneries of corrugated iron, honky tonks, restaurants, and whore houses, and little crowded groceries, and laboratories and flophouses.

36. When George Gerard Egan served as selectman of Madison, Connecticut, he would call important messages early in the morning he thought that time the best because people were usually home.

37. After Joe Guglielmo threw a knuckle ball on a three and two count to the most dangerous hitter in Holy Cross baseball history.

38. Doctor Mark Catania, an expert on the science of catching bluefish, tells everyone how to catch the choppers he never hesitates to tell an adjacent fisherman what is wrong.

39. Pat and Don Williams sailed the New England Coast, docked at Newport, Rhode Island, and ordered a huge lobster from Dave at the Aquidneck Lobster Company.

40. Because Gerd and Dave Nelson excepted the offer from the hotel chain, they now have a condo in Manhattan to visit every year for a week.

41. Richard Henry Bornemann is the only person I know whom is conversant in both art and music and speaks sixteen languages.

42. As the data were recovered, the F.B.I. slowly put the facts together to convict several company presidents.

43. After a tragic occurrence, one should keep busy by traveling, by writing to relatives, and by pursuing avocations. This will take the mind away from sadness, according to Claire Kerrigan.

44. Ben Kupcho used to give the best grades to whomever scored the highest on the standardized tests.

45. If the principal and the vice-principal makes a decision regarding a recalcitrant student, he should definitely notify the parents of the situation.

46. We were told after the game the bonfire, scheduled for nine, would be postponed until the next week.

47. On the day after the long night of September 11, after we had called our families to say that we were alive, after we had walked the midnight streets and filed our newspaper stories, after we had watched television until four in the morning, after some

broken hours of jagged sleep, my wife and I went out together to see the changed world.

48. Hurricane Katrina in 2005 devastated New Orleans, caused prices of fuel to double, and to many it was the worst disaster in American history.

49. If everyone took care of their own problems, psychiatrists would be out of business.

50. Vera and Don Perry, along with a relative who spoke five languages, travels to Europe several times a year on business.

ANSWERS

1. Dangling modifier. If Paul Michael Randall were wriggling back and forth, he could not catch the snake any way. To correct, add "wriggling back and forth" after "snake."

2. Ambiguous reference. The pronoun "he" refers to both Brian Mark Randall *and* his brother. Change the sentence to read as follows: "BMR said to his brother, 'Get ready to meet Magic Johnson.'"

3. Parallel structure mistake. "Dabbled" should be "dabbling."

4. Mixing active and passive voice in the same sentence. Possible correction: ". . . lakefront; the Garden Club of Western Connecticut asked him to join its ranks."

5. Correct, even though far-fetched.

6. Misplaced modifier. "Only" should be placed after "take."

7. Agreement of subject and verb. The verb should be "goes" to agree with the singular subject and is not affected by the words set off by commas.

8. Commas missing. There should be one after "Krause" and one after "traveler"; appositives are set off by commas.

9. Incorrect coordination. "And" should be "but" to convey the correct meaning.

10. Parallel structure mistake. "Writes" should be "wrote" and "cause" should be "caused."

11. Correct.

12. Usage problem. "Beside" should have an s at the end.

13. Usage again. "Into" should be used in place of "in."

14. Fragment. Usually a fragment of any kind can be attached to an existing sentence to make sense. By adding a sentence to this fragment, commas should be added: "If only Dean Harold Zanardi, when he paved the Mulvey's driveway in the middle of a July heatwave, had mentioned that a car should not be used on the new pavement, there would not be the ruts that suddenly appeared."

15. General reference of the pronoun "which." Change "which" to "These talents" and put a period after "neighbors."

16. Correct.

17. Weak reference. "One" does not take the place of anything. Use "a tray" or "a bus bucket."

18. Misplaced modifier. Although Joe is big enough to swing an attic, the sentence should read as follows: "In his attic, JB found a bat he used to swing when he was younger."

19. Usage problem. Obviously, "adapted" should be "adopted."

20. Comma problem. One is needed after "profession." Introductory adverb clauses need commas to set them off at the beginning of a sentence.

21. Parallel structure error. After "company" place the second correlative conjunction "but also"; then, eliminate the "also" after the word "money."

22. Agreement of pronoun and antecedent. "He" could refer to either Gates or Purcell. There is also a problem with "his." Change the sentence to read as follows: ". . . he had no idea of Tom's arrest . . . ."

23. Agreement of subject and verb. Because of the conjunction "or," the verb must agree with the closest subject—"some." Change "is" to "are."

24. Correct.

25. General reference of the pronoun "it." Change "it was" to "these actions were."

26. Ambiguous reference. Too many pronouns to begin with. Also, the verb "would" seems not to make sense. A suggested correction: ". . . said that Kyle should . . . ."

27. Correct.

28. Parallel structure. After "or," the second part of the correlative conjunction, change the words to read: "to stay home . . . ."

29. Usage error. "Reason" and "because" are redundant. Change "because" to "that."

30. Past participle error. "Casted" should be "cast" and "like" should be "as if."

31. Capital letters missing. Personification of seasons demands that they be capitalized. Thus, "Summer" and "Spring."

32. Run-on sentence. After "Luncheonette," a semicolon is needed, or put a period to create two sentences. Add commas after "politics" and "Roadkill."

33. Agreement of subject and verb. A singular subject follows "or" and demands that "prove" be "proves." You might want to throw a comma after "teacher"; also, "their" should be "one's" or "his."

34. Correct. A sentence from *Cannery Row* by John Steinbeck.

35. Correct. Another sentence from *Cannery Row*.

36. Run-on. Put a semicolon after "morning." By the way, this sentence is true. I once received a phone call from George at five in the morning.

37. Fragment. I was catching when Joe threw the ball. I'll finish the sentence: ". . . history, a gigantic home run occurred." (It was still rising when it went over the 410 sign down the left field line.)

38. Run-on. Put a semicolon after "choppers."

39. Correct. Dave knows how to pick them.

40. Usage mistake. "Excepted" should be "accepted."

41. Usage—incorrect case of relative pronoun. "Whom" should be "who."

42. Correct. "Data" is plural.

43. General reference of pronouns. "This" should be changed to "These activities."

44. Incorrect case. "Whomever" should be "whoever" because it is the subject of the clause.

45. Ambiguous reference. The reader cannot tell to whom "he" refers. Also, the verb "makes" should read "make" because of the plural subject. Suggested correction: ". . . student, the parents should be notified immediately."

46. Misplaced modifier. "After the game" is in the wrong place. Put "after the game" before "we" and the problem is solved.

47. Correct. I borrowed this sentence from Pete Hamill's *Downtown, My Manhattan*. I met Pete at R. J. Julia's, a great bookstore in Madison, Connecticut.

48. Parallel structure. After "double," put the following: ". . . and ranks as one of the worst natural disasters in American history."

49. Agreement of pronoun and antecedent. "Everyone" is singular so that "their" should read "his" or "her." To avoid the gender gaffe, use "individuals" instead of "everyone" so that "their" would be correct.

50. Agreement of subject and verb. "Travels" should be "travel."

APPENDICES

The Truth must dazzle gradually
Or every man be blind—

Emily Dickinson

Appendix One

Pronouns and Helping Verbs

Personal Pronouns

Subjective Pronouns (use as subjects and predicate pronouns)

Singular	Plural
I	we
you	you
he, she, it	they

Objective Pronouns (use as objects of the preposition, direct object, indirect object)

Singular	Plural
me	us
you	you
him, her, it	them

Possessive Pronouns (use to show possession— NO APOSTROPHES)

Singular	Plural
my, mine	our, ours
your, yours	your, yours
his, her, hers, its	their, theirs

INDEFINITE PRONOUNS

Singular		**Plural**	**Singular or Plural**
another	much	both	all
anybody	neither	few	any
anyone	nobody	many	more
anything	no one	others	most
each	nothing	several	none
either	one		some
everybody	other		half
everyone	somebody		enough
everything	someone		
little	something		

DEMONSTRATIVE PRONOUNS

that	this
these	those

RELATIVE PRONOUNS

that	who	whose
which	whom	

HELPING VERBS

be	do	have	can
is	does	has	could
am	did	had	may
are			might
was			must
were			shall
been			should
			will
			would

Appendix Two

TRANSITIONAL EXPRESSIONS

Transitional expressions make writing smooth and understandable. The careful writer uses these words or groups of words sparingly and strategically to bridge ideas within sentences, between sentences, within paragraphs, and between paragraphs. The following examples also show the purposes for which some expressions can be used. Although not a complete list (Writers sometimes have their own expressions), I'm sure this section will help coordinate ideas.

Purpose	Transitional Expressions
to time	after a while, afterward, at once, again, at that time, at last, as long as, at length, before, besides, earlier (later), eventually, finally, formerly, further, furthermore, first (second, third, . . .), in addition, in the first place, in the past, last, lately, here, meanwhile, next, now, presently, shortly, thereafter, subsequently, until, soon, still, until now, when
to position	above, across from, around, before, beyond, here, nearby, to my left, to my right, above me, below me, opposite to, adjacent to, under, under me, in the background, close at hand
to add or expound	again, also, and, another, besides, further, furthermore, moreover, next, finally, too, last, first, in the first place, similarly, likewise, in the same way, in addition

to compare	also, in the same way, likewise, similarly, in the same manner
to contrast	although, however, nevertheless, but, yet, nor, on the contrary, instead, in spite of, on the other hand (five fingers), regardless (no such word as "irregardless"), otherwise, though, in contrast, notwithstanding, even though, even so, conversely, at the same time, simultaneously
to illustrate or exemplify	for example, for instance, to illustrate, as an illustration, that is, even, in short, in conclusion, it is true, of course, namely
to conclude	therefore, as a result, thus, consequently, finally, as a consequence, in conclusion, for this (these) reason(s)
to summarize	in conclusion, to sum up, to recap, to conclude, as I have said, therefore, in brief, in fact, in any case
to emphasize	to repeat, again, for this (these) purpose(s), with this (these) points in mind, most important(ly), least important(ly)

Appendix Three

IRREGULAR VERBS

Present	Past	Past Participle	Present Participle
arise	arose	arisen	arising
awake	awoke or awaked	awoken or awaked	awaking
bear	bore	borne or born	bearing
beat	beat	beaten or beat	beating
become	became	become	becoming
begin	began	begun	beginning
bend	bent	bent	bending
bet	bet or betted	bet or betted	betting
bind	bound	bound	binding
bite	bit	bitten or bit	biting
bleed	bled	bled	bleeding
blow	blew	blown	blowing
break	broke	broken	breaking
breed	bred	bred	breeding
build	built	built	building
buy	bought	bought	buying
catch	caught	caught	catching
choose	chose	chosen	choosing
cling	clung	clung	clinging
come	came	come	coming
creep	crept	crept	creeping
cut	cut	cut	cutting
deal	dealt	dealt	dealing
dig	dug	dug	digging
dive	dived or dove	dived or dove	diving
do	did	done	doing
draw	drew	drawn	drawing
dream	dreamed or dreamt	dreamed or dreamt	dreaming
drink	drank	drunk or drank	drinking

Present	Past	Past Participle	Present Participle
eat	ate	eaten	eating
fall	fell	fallen	falling
feed	fed	fed	feeding
feel	felt	felt	feeling
fight	fought	fought	fighting
find	found	found	finding
flee	fled	fled	fleeing
fling	flung	flung	flinging
fly	flew	flown	flying
forbid	forbade or forbad	forbidden	forbidding
forget	forgot	forgot	forgetting
forget	forgot	forgotten	forgetting
forgive	forgave	forgiven	forgiving
freeze	froze	frozen	freezing
get	got	gotten or got	getting
give	gave	given	giving
go	went	gone	going
grind	ground	ground	grinding
grow	grew	grown	growing
hang (suspend)	hung	hung	hanging
hang (from a rope)	hanged	hanged	hanging (regular verb)
have	had	had	having
hear	heard	heard	hearing
hide	hid	hidden or hid	hiding
hold	held	held	holding
hurt	hurt	hurt	hurting
keep	kept	kept	keeping
know	knew	known	knowing
lay	laid	laid	laying
lead	led	led	leading
leave	left	left	leaving
lend	lent	lent	lending
let	let	let	letting
lie	lay	lain	lying
lose	lost	lost	losing

Present	Past	Past Participle	Present Participle
make	made	made	making
mean	meant	meant	meaning
meet	met	met	meeting
pay	paid	paid	paying
prove	proved	proved or proven	proving
put	put	put	putting
putt (in golf)	putted	putted	putting (regular verb)
quit	quit	quit	quitting
read	read	read	reading
ride	rode	ridden	riding
ring	rang	rung	ringing
rise	rose	risen	rising
run	ran	run	running
saw	sawed	sawed or sawn	sawing
say	said	said	saying
see	saw	seen	seeing
seek	sought	sought	seeking
sell	sold	sold	selling
send	sent	sent	sending
set	set	set	setting
shake	shook	shaken	shaking
shed	shed	shed	shedding
shine	shone or shined	shone or shined	shining
shoe	shod or shoed	shod or shoe	shoeing
shoot	shot	shot	shooting
show	showed	showed or shown	showing
shrink	shrank or shrunk	shrunk or shrunken	shrinking
shut	shut	shut	shutting
sing	sang	sung	singing
sink	sank or sunk	sunk	sinking
sit	sat	sat	sitting
slay	slew (slayed)	slain	slaying
sleep	slept	slept	sleeping
slide	slid	slid	sliding
sling	slung	slung	slinging
smell	smelled or smelt	smelled or smelt	smelling

Present	Past	Past Participle	Present Participle
smite	smote	smitten	smiting
speak	spoke	spoken	speaking
spend	spent	spent	spending
spin	spun	spun	spinning
spread	spread	spread	spreading
spring	sprang	sprung	springing
stand	stood	stood	standing
steal	stole	stolen	stealing
stick	stuck	stuck	sticking
sting	stung	stung	stinging
stink	stank or stunk	stunk	stinking
strike	struck	struck or stricken	striking
string	strung	strung	stringing
strive	strove	striven	striving
swear	swore	sworn	swearing
sweep	swept	swept	sweeping
swim	swam	swum	swimming
swing	swung	swung	swinging
take	took	taken	taking
teach	taught	taught	teaching
tear	tore	torn	tearing
tell	told	told	telling
think	thought	thought	thinking

Appendix Four

CONJUGATION OF IRREGULAR VERBS

Active Indicative

Present

I throw

you throw

he, she, it throws

we throw

you throw

they throw

Past

I arose

you arose

he, she, it arose

we arose

you arose

they arose

Future

I will build

you will build

he, she, it will build

we will build

you will build

they will build

Present Perfect

I have dragged

you have dragged

he, she, it has dragged

we have dragged

you have dragged

they have dragged

Past Perfect

I had caught

you had caught

he, she, it had caught

we had caught

you had caught

they had caught

Future Perfect

I will have fought

you will have fought

he, she, it will have fought

we will have fought

you will have fought

they will have fought

Indicative Passive

Present
I am chosen
you are chosen
he, she, it is chosen

we are chosen
you are chosen
they are chosen

Past
I was found
you were found
he, she, it, was found

we were found
you were found
they were found

Future
I will be beaten
you will be beaten
he, she, it will be beaten

we will be beaten
you will be beaten
they will be beaten

Present Perfect
I have been shot
you have been shot
he, she, it has been shot

we have been shot
you have been shot
they have been shot

Past Perfect
I had been stung
you had been stung
he, she, it had been stung

we had been stung
you had been stung
they had been stung

Future Perfect
I will have been struck
you will have been struck
he, she, it will have been struck

we will have been struck
you will have been struck
they will have been struck

Progressive (active—always)

Present
I am throwing
you are throwing
he, she, it is throwing

we are throwing
you are throwing
they are throwing

Past
I was thinking
you were thinking
he, she, it was thinking

we were thinking
you were thinking
they were thinking

Future

I will be standing	we will be standing
you will be standing	you will be standing
he, she, it will be standing	they will be standing

Present Perfect

I have been shaking	we have been shaking
you have been shaking	you have been shaking
he, she, it has been shaking	they have been shaking

Past Perfect

I had been writing	we had been writing
you had been writing	you had been writing
he had been writing	they had been writing

Future Perfect

I will have been swimming	we will have been swimming
you will have been swimming	you will have been swimming
he, she, it will have been swimming	they will have been swimming

Emphatic (present and past only)

Present

I do fight	we do fight
you do fight	you do fight
he, she, it does fight	they do fight

Past

I did choose	we did choose
you did choose	you did choose
he, she, it, did choose	they did choose

Subjunctive (present with any verb; and past only with were)

Present

I find	we find
you find	you find
he, she, it finds	they find

Past

I were	we were
you were	you were
he, she, it were	they were

Appendix Five

LIST OF PREPOSITIONS

abeam	beyond	since	according to
about	by	through	because of
above	down	throughout	by way of
across	during	till	in addition to
after	except	to	in front of
against	for	toward	in place of
among	from	under	in regard to
around	in	until	in spite of
as	inside	up	instead of
at	into	upon	on account of
athwart	like	with	out of
before	near	without	with regard to
behind	of		
below	off		
beneath	on		
beside	out		
besides	outside		
between	over		

TIDBITS

ENGLISH IS EASY?

Read the following sentences carefully:

1. "Get the <u>lead</u> out so that you can <u>lead</u>," said Catherine Welch.
2. Because he was an <u>invalid</u>, his insurance policy was <u>invalid</u>.
3. The custodian told the tenant he would <u>refuse</u> to take the <u>refuse</u> to the dump.
4. The <u>does</u> followed the skunk when it <u>does</u> some spraying.
5. Shauna tends to <u>read</u> what her father has <u>read</u>.
6. The <u>sewer</u> watched as her needle and thread fell into the <u>sewer</u>.
7. When Dean Bennett saw the <u>tear</u> in the new Picasso, he shed a <u>tear</u>.
8. The <u>wind</u> prevented us from <u>wind</u>ing the kite string.
9. The heat in the <u>desert</u> caused the general to <u>desert</u> just before <u>dessert</u> was served.

10. The <u>sow</u> in the sty was <u>so</u> thin that its owner was forced to <u>sow</u> more grain.

11. To <u>close</u> the <u>closet</u> door when you're <u>close</u> to the <u>clothes</u> inside is impossible.

12. The surgeon <u>wound</u> the <u>wound</u> with duct tape.

13. If the <u>bee</u> were quicker, he would <u>be</u> alive; he's <u>been</u> dead awhile.

14. The <u>dove</u> <u>dove</u> at the bug.

15. Pat Clifford said, "I <u>object</u> to that <u>object</u> used as evidence."

16. The striped <u>bass</u>, if he could sing, would be a <u>bass</u> or <u>bass</u>o.

17. The precious <u>present</u> was <u>present</u>ed to everyone <u>present</u>.

18. The bishop began to <u>see</u> that his <u>see</u> was crumbling.

19. The mortician <u>passed</u> the casket <u>past</u> the mourners.

20. The hunter from <u>Butte</u>, Montana, was a <u>beaut</u>.

21. The <u>deer</u> was a <u>dear</u>.

22. Margaret MacGruer tried to <u>console</u> her husband who had dropped the <u>console</u>.

23. Mike Maney shot a <u>bow</u> from the <u>bow</u> of the ship and later took a <u>bow</u>.

24. Sue Maney was not <u>content</u> with the <u>content</u> of the book she was reading.

25. The <u>convict</u> could not understand why some could <u>convict</u> him of the crime.

26. The <u>buffet</u> was interrupted because of the <u>buffet</u>ing of the wind.

27. The <u>minute</u> particles took a <u>minute</u> to see.

28. My uncle used to <u>separate</u> the magazines into <u>separate</u> piles.

29. "If you <u>do</u> not wish to sing <u>do</u>," said the music teacher, "please sing <u>mi</u> for <u>me</u>."

30. I drank some <u>sake</u> for my wife's <u>sake</u>.

TWO SYLLABLES, ADD TWO LETTERS— ONE SYLLABLE

Another oddity. What two-syllable, four-letter word becomes a one-syllable word after adding two letters? The word is *ague*. Add *pl* and *plague* appears. This language is easy.

Scientific . . . but

"Aquatic Nuisance Species lists should not include all non-native or invasive species. The term 'nuisance' **infers** that they are non-native to a region or habitat, undesirable and require action."

from a report from the Connecticut Aquatic Nuisance Species Management

So maybe **implies** is non-technical language.

Even Yankee Announcers Commit Language Errors

During a game against the Orioles on June 27, 2005, Ken Singleton, one of the Yankee announcers said about Carl Pavano: ". . . and the walk **exasperates** things . . . ." Now there is nothing worse than an **exasperated thing.** I'll bet he meant to say "**exacerbated** things."

Not a Dickinson Word

On June 29, 2005, on the *Today* Show, John Watters, talking about credit card fraud and how "phishers" (con men) use personal information, said, "We don't know how **impactful** it can be." Now there's a word you can take your hat off to—and then smash it on the ground.

Bob's Cheap Furniture Language

In an ad (talking about mattresses) on TV for Bob's Furniture, written on the screen: "Will their's last longer?" I forget. Is it *Bobs* or *Bob's*? Is it *theirs* or *their's*."

Carl Sandburg's "Hangman at Home"
Or "anything is a subject for poetry"

What does the hangman think about
When he goes home at night from work?
When he sits down with his wife and
Children for a cup of coffee and a
Plate of ham and eggs, do they ask
Him if it was a good day's work
And everything went well or do they
Stay off some topics, and talk about
The weather, baseball, politics,
And the comic strips in the papers
And the movies? Do they look at his
Hands when he reaches for the coffee
Or the ham and eggs? If the little
Ones say, Daddy, play horse, here's
A rope—does he answer like a joke:
I seen enough rope for today?
Or does his face light up like a
Bonfire of joy and does he say:
It's a good and dandy world we live
In. And if a white face moon looks
In through a window where a baby girl
Sleeps and the moon gleams mix with
Baby ears and baby hair—the hangman—
How does he act then? It must be easy
For him. Anything is easy for a hangman,
I guess.

Pet Language Peeve

Lately I have noticed that when I say "Thank you" to someone, even one my age, the person responds, "No problem!" However, there was not a problem in the first place.

As a side note: Why don't clerks in stores count change back to you? They look at the register, say "Your change is (whatever)," and hand you coins and bills. Regardless of the size of the line, I count the money—slowly.

Then there's "Go ahead and . . ." or, "You need to . . ."—redundancies everyone can do without.

Misuse of the Appositive

From the *New Haven Register*, Friday, December 10, 2004: "Always a sharp dresser, Superintendent of Schools H. Kaye Griffin's biggest problem this week as she prepares for a trip to China . . . ." Now, the writer intended to refer to Ms. Griffin as the "sharp dresser," but since H. Kaye Griffin becomes an adjective with the *'s*, dresser refers to the word "problem." No problem.

A Simile (and a Smile) for Football Fans

This is from an unidentified radio announcer at a Michigan–Ohio State game. He is referring to an Ohio State back as he "ran through the MSU line like Mexican water through a first-time tourist."

From the Internet

Thursday, October 13, 2005—Ronald Blum, AP sportswriter, on Mel Stottlemyre's leaving the Yankees: "Stottlemyre has threatened to leave after several seasons but came back each time. He said the second-guessing [of Steinbrenner] had a 'cumulative' **affect** over the years."

Maybe Mel did say "affect," but I doubt it.

SUPERWOMAN DOES NOT EXIST

My good friend Kippy Martin wrote *Superwoman Does Not Exist*. She calls herself my second oldest student (she's in her early forties and can outrun the high school track team); here are two pieces from her work:

> I keep telling my husband that I'm the Playwoman—I'm not trying to do it all. The woman he thinks I am can be found on television—the woman who handles working inside and outside the home, and wears a size five dress above the knee. The house is spotless, dinner is always prepared on time, and the family cheery and presentable. I call her the Soap Opera Woman.

> *and*

> I realized that going to the best graduate school could not help me with parenting and marital skills. I had to call up the School of Reality where Grandmothers are presidents, Moms are vice presidents, and Fathers are consultants on providing strategies for their daughters.

I LOVE IMUS IN THE MORNING

The Don Imus Show ranks as one of my favorite radio programs. Not only does it feature guests such as Richard Nixon, Mike Tyson, and writers from *Newsweek* and *Time*, but I can always count on the misuse of words from Imus and crew (with the exception of Charles McCord).

> Tuesday, January 25, 2005—Imus: "Wyatt said to his mother and I that he wanted to adopt . . . ."
>
> *and*
>
> Bernie: He should have **threw** the dog out the window.

Two Bush (League) Errors on the Same Day

In reference to a breaking news story about whether to feed a patient through tubes or let her die, brothers Bush, George W. and Jeb, the Governor of Florida, on television mispronounced "err" to rhyme with "air."

> George W: "We should "air" on the side of life . . . ."
> Jeb: "We should "air" on the side of protecting her . . . ."

Same speech writer?

The Five-Paragraph Blunder

In the back of my mind I remember hearing an English teacher say that the five-paragraph essay was an excellent assignment because it was easy to correct. I looked further into this new reinvention of writing, tried it once, and then vowed that I would never assign it to any of my classes.

First, it stifles creativity. Who said that an essay should start with a topic sentence? Whoever mandated that an essay end with a concluding sentence? And who demanded that an essay be limited to just five paragraphs? I choose, then, three of my favorite essays from

Ralph Waldo Emerson to emphasize that the topic sentence may not always be the first sentence of an essay. I'm sure Mr. Emerson turned over in his grave when the five-paragraph essay was introduced. (He actually did disinter his first wife because he wanted to see death firsthand; why would not he turn over in death?)

Here are the opening sentences of "Self-Reliance," "Friendship," and "Nature."

> **From "Self-Reliance":** I read the other day some verses written by an eminent painter which were original and not conventional.
>
> **From "Friendship":** We have a great deal more kindness than is ever spoken.
>
> **From "Nature":** There are days which occur in this climate, at almost any season of the year, wherein the world reaches its perfection, when the air, the heavenly bodies, and the earth, make a harmony, as if nature would indulge her offspring; when, in these bleak upper sides of the planet, nothing is to desire that we have heard of the happiest latitudes, and we bask in the shining hours of Florida and Cuba; when everything that has life gives sign of satisfaction, and the cattle that lit on the ground seem to have great and tranquil thoughts.

I dare you to read the rest of these essays.

YANKEES MISSING ANTECEDENT

From the *Times*, Thursday, September 22, 2005, an article by Jack Curry:

> "The Yankees barely needed to save Johnson last night [he was thrown out of the game in his previous start] as

he maintained his composure and stifled the Baltimore Orioles in a 2–1 victory at Yankee Stadium. Other than mimicking Miguel Tejada's check swing to try to convince the first-base umpire that **he** had swung, Johnson was as reserved as a mannequin in eight sturdy innings."

Number one, I don't remember umpires ever getting to the plate. Number two, how could Randy Johnson possibly hit one of his own fastballs. Number three, "he" refers to Miguel Tejada—but the writer turned him into an adjective, which, in this case, can't have an antecedent. Number four, as long as we're being picky, "reserved" hardly applies to the mannequins in Bloomingdale's—the ones sporting sexy bathing suits.

Garmin Garble

With a new GPS, I am forced to read technical language—not one of my fortes. While learning how to convert TD's (time differences) into latitude and longitude, I came across two beauts of errors on page 3 of *Garmin Loran TD Position Format Handbook*:

1. "After a Master Station transmits **it's** pulsed RF signal . . . ." (word choice)
2. "From those three signals, a set of two TD's are constructed and **using the TD's** a location can be plotted." (dangling modifier)

Appendix Seven

GLOSSARY OF TERMS USED (WITH ALTERNATE EXPLANATIONS AND EXAMPLES)

Abstract Noun Nouns that are more imagined than seen. Integrity may be seen by one's actions, but you cannot see an integrity. Other examples: *abstemiousness, wrath, crapulousness, capriciousness*.

Active Voice The active voice, with the verb, tells the reader what the subject of the sentence is doing.

> *Stephan Allis* <u>writes</u> speeches for Washington politicians.
>
> *Clayborn Cowin Rich* <u>owns</u> more tractors than the entire John Deere Company.

Adjective, One Word An adjective is used to describe, modify, change, or limit a noun. Notice how "fishing boat" is changed by adding some words and limiting the boat in question to one particular craft: <u>Single-engine</u>, <u>twenty-two-foot</u>, <u>inboard</u> <u>wooden</u> fishing boat.

Adjective Phrase A group of words, which does not contain a verb, that describes, limits, modifies, or somehow changes a noun (or pronoun). Notice the underlined parts and how they add something to another word, usually a noun or pronoun:

Smiling prettily and working efficiently, Kelly McManus and Laura Hutton work long hours at the Madison Country Club.

Karen Louise Caturano thought that the décor in St. Mary's basement resembled the ballroom at the Waldorf Astoria.

Adjective Clause A group of words containing a subject and verb. This group functions just like the ONE-WORD ADJECTIVE or ADJECTIVE PHRASE by limiting, describing, modifying, or sometimes changing a noun or pronoun:

Jared Joseph Silva, who claims he can spell any word in the English language, will certainly receive a scholarship to college.

Dynamite, a forty-foot Luhrs that does not catch any fish, should be renamed *Conservation*.

Adverb, One Word A word that describes, limits, modifies, or somehow changes a verb, adjective, or even another adverb.

Changing a verb: Joel Daniel Silva skips jauntily to school.

Changing an adjective: June in 2005 became <u>extremely</u> hot.

Changing another adverb (which may never be needed): Jenna Lee Silva becomes <u>overly</u> excited when she watches the "Flintstones."

Adverb Phrase A group of words, without a subject and verb, that modifies, describes, limits, or somehow changes a verb or an adjective. I have yet to see an adverb phrase modify another adverb.

Adverb phrase with a verb: Peter Francis Palmieri *caught,* <u>in three consecutive seasons</u>, more fish than anyone else in Newington.

<u>To insure a trip to Foxwoods</u>, Brenda Lou Laperuta *plied* Peter Francis with several cocktails.

Adverb phrase with an adjective: *Lost* <u>in the labyrinth</u> of the mall, Jack Sprat Lamson wandered aimlessly until found.

Catherine Welch was *reluctant* <u>to speak to her mentor</u>.

Adverb Clause A group of words with a subject and verb that modifies, changes, limits, or describes the action of a noun (mainly) or the status of an adjective or even another adverb.

Adverb clause with a verb: <u>Because Dr. Tom Suchanek travels frequently</u>, he *has amassed* thousands of frequent flier miles.

Adverb clause with an adjective: Gwen Goodman, now a lawyer, showed that she was as *intelligent* <u>as a doctor is</u> when she aided the traffic accident victim.

Adverb clause with another adverb: Walter Falkoff <u>arises</u> every morning *as happily as a pig is* because he is about to lead another happy customer to rainbow trout the size of alligators.

Agreement The subject must *agree* with the verb and the pronoun must *agree* with the noun. All this means is that the number (singular or plural) must be the same.

> Priscilla Boullie Rich (singular) bakes (singular) the best pies in the western hemisphere.
>
> Leslie Donkin and Lauren Blumann (plural) were (plural) the best students at Hand High School.
>
> Everyone (singular) should bring her (singular) own costume to the Halloween party.

Antecedent A noun (or pronoun) that refers to another pronoun.

> *Ronald J. Dziema* brought <u>his</u> boat to <u>his</u> lakefront cottage.
>
> *Pamela Rich Mulhearn* and *John William Mulhearn* own <u>their</u> home.

Appositive (one word or compound noun) An appositive is a noun that immediately follows another noun and renames it. The purpose is to emphasize the previous noun.

> *Mark Brennan*, <u>author</u>, visits the bartender at Lynch's every Sunday.

Appositives can be phrases also.

> *Janet Ellen Violissi*, <u>the proprietor of The Historic Killingworth Inn</u>, doubles as a Notary Public and a Justice of the Peace.

Notice the way in which the underlined parts add to the names.

> <u>Tinky Dakota Weisblat and her neighbor</u> (plural) chair the annual Pudding Contest in Claremont, Massachusetts, and they (plural) share the results with the world.

Clause A group of words that contain a subject and verb and functions as a noun, adjective, or adverb.

> **Noun Clause:** <u>Whatever Brendan Rich Mulhearn wanted for Christmas</u> he received. (noun clause used as a direct object of "received")
>
> **Adjective Clause:** Sarah Talbert Behringer wants to own a horse <u>that will take her on journeys</u> <u>through the woods.</u> (adjective clause modifying "horse")
>
> **Adverb Clause:** <u>Whenever Alexander Scott Behringer went downtown</u>, he would buy a lollypop. (adverb clause modifying "would buy")

Collective Noun A noun that "gathers" individuals. Usually singular in nature, these nouns make one see groups of geese (skein when they're flying; gaggle when they're messing up the ground), schools of fish or kiddies, prides of lions, coalitions of cheetahs, and bloats of hippopotami.

Common Noun A noun that is generic and not usually capitalized: *dog, cat, man, woman.*

Concrete Noun A noun that has visible or felt substance: *book, lamp, sun, radio, chart.*

Conjunction A word or two that join two other parts of a sentence. See COORDINATING CONJUNCTIONS and CORRELATIVE CONJUNCTIONS.

Coordinating Conjunctions They are *and, but, or, nor, for, yet*. They join words, phrases, clauses, or sentences:

> Kathy Filosi *and* Pat Raudat call each other often. (joining words)
>
> *Composing crossword puzzles, building his dream house,* and *involving himself* in civic affairs, Joe Venuti keeps busy. (joining phrases)
>
> Eleanor Montgomery, *who lives in North Attleboro* and *who babysits her grandchildren often,* used to hit the longest home runs seen by anyone in Madison. (joining clauses)
>
> *Fran Hall worked as a nurse for thirty years,* yet *she always had time to visit relatives in Florida.* (joining sentences)

Correlative Conjunctions They are *either . . . or, neither . . . nor, not only . . . but also, whether . . . or, both . . . and*. Each joins like grammatical terms.

> *Both* Gail *and* Jimmy Lester have roots in Madison, Connecticut. (two nouns joined)
>
> Barbara Steinberg *not only* promotes civic activities *but also* joins creditable organizations. (two verbs joined)

Countable Noun These nouns usually can be pluralized with *-s* or *-es* and can be defined with "a" or "an": *a coupon, imps, an imposter, players, an act.*

Compound Noun A noun made up of two or more words. These may be hyphenated or not, separated or not: *ham and eggs, mainstream, mother-in-law*

Complex Sentence "Complex," in this case, does not mean intricate or deep. It means simply that a sentence contains <u>one</u>

main clause, a sentence, and at least *one dependent clause*, a clause that cannot stand by itself and mean something.

> *Whenever Kerin Cole Mulhearn speaks,* <u>people listen</u>.
>
> <u>Jill Rich Behringer thought</u> *that her father had too many toys after she inspected the barn.*

Compound Sentence A compound sentence contains two (or more) main clauses. In other words, it combines two or more simple sentences. Compound sentences can be punctuated in different ways.

> Ibrahim V. Shareef works at least two jobs, and he never seems to be tired.
>
> Kathleen Leisure looked for a teaching position in New York City; she had a difficult decision to make.
>
> William Francis Gashlin helps others steer correctly; in addition, Megan Rose Lynch steers William correctly.

Compound Complex Sentence This type of sentence comprises two (or more) <u>main clauses</u> and at least one (or more) *dependent clauses*.

> <u>Richard Henry Bornemann</u>, *who writes speeches for politicians,* <u>roots for the Boston Red Sox</u>, and <u>his friend Dan</u>, *who likes the Mets,* <u>writes nasty letters to the editors of local newspapers.</u>
>
> *While Taylor Priscilla Mulhearn plays the piano,* <u>Scott Thomas Behringer accompanies her on the flute</u>, but <u>no one else in the</u> family <u>has a propensity for music.</u>

Conjunction This word or words connect. Also, they build a relationship between words, between phrases, between clauses, and between sentences. The one-word conjunctions are *and, but, or, not for, yet*. These words need commas when they join two sentences. When they join two words or phrases or subordinate clauses, a comma is needed only if they are joining more than two items. The correlative conjunctions, made up of two related words, are *either . . . or, neither . . . nor, not only . . . but also, whether . . . or, both . . . and*. These usually do not require commas.

> Doug "The Chief" Macdonald frequently travels to Rome, *yet* he prefers Liars Saloon in Montauk over any Italian trattoria.
>
> *Both* Eddie Kendall *and* Big Walt fish Long Island Sound.
>
> *Either* Clement P. Kerley is working as a strategic management advisor *or* he is writing plays and novels with interesting themes.

Dangling Modifier The word "dangling" sticks in everyone's mind, but ask someone what it is and he will guess. Briefly, it is any kind of modifier that does not sensibly relate to what it's supposed to.

> Dressed only in her nightclothes, the bear scared Jessica Loring Behringer and her camping buddies out of their tents. (As you can see, the nightclothes belong to Jessica—unless the bear is making a fashion statement.)
>
> To follow the law properly, illegal porgies cannot be used to catch larger species. (Here, we have the "illegal porgies" following the law properly. Porgies are great bait stealers but are hardly able to reason.)

Demonstrative Pronoun These are *this, that, these*, and *those*. They seem to demonstrate or point out something as in *that chair* or *these books*. *This* and *that* should be used only with singular nouns; *these* and *those* should be used only with plural nouns.

> Lee A. Jacobus, Professor of English Emiritus, once said, "*This* library is one of the best" referring to the Clinton, Connecticut, library off Route 81.

> Monsignor Gerard Gaynor Schmitz, who loves a good meal, once said at a table, "*These* beans are the best I have ever tasted."

Dependent Clause Either an adjective, adverb, or noun, these clauses have a subject and verb but cannot stand alone as a sentence. They need to be attached to a complete sentence to make sense. They add information to the existing words, but these clauses, mostly, could just as well be reworded into a word or phrase.

> Joseph Gregory Murphy, who preaches at St. Margaret in Madison, Connecticut, spends hours on his sermons. (Sometimes we do not need to know where he preaches so that the sentence could read more simply.)

> J. G. M., a preacher, spends hours on his sermons.

Direct Object A noun (and therefore a word, a phrase, or a clause) or pronoun that receives (much like a tight end) something (ball) from the action (throws) from the subject (quarterback) and verb (throws).

> **Word:** Jonathan Meyers (quarterback) writes (throws) scripts (ball) for television in Florida.

> **Phrase:** Don Snow (quarterback) loves (throws) playing (ball) tennis at the Beach Club.

> **Clause:** Kim Blondin (quarterback) reads (throws) whatever she gets her hands on (ball).

Emphatic Mood The verb *do* and its parts emphasize so that when you say something like "I did build that bridge," you are in the emphatic mood.

> Cindy Hoover once said that she *did* like the people in Madison.

Fragment This error, sometimes acceptable in poetry and fiction, rarely is acceptable in standard written English. A fragment is part of a sentence written as if it were a sentence: That is, it will begin with a capital letter and end in a period.

> First.
>
> First and foremost.
>
> Whatever Thomas Mesner cooks.
>
> Joseph Brandi, Jr., who is responsible for some of the best dishes seen around the shoreline.

Correction of a fragment is easy. Just attach it to a sentence.

General Reference of Pronouns Many writers do not consider this error an error. I do. General reference occurs when a pronoun such as *it*, *which*, *that*, or *this* refers to a general idea.

> *It* bothers me that some writers consider fragments, run-ons, and slang part of standard written (and spoken) English.
>
> Bob Harris tried to sell me a car with electric windows, air conditioning, leather bucket seats, dual airbags, a DVD player, an extra set of tires, and a lifetime warranty on all parts. *This* led me to another choice.

Indefinite Pronoun These pronouns refer to nothing in particular and therefore are "indefinite." See Appendix One for an almost complete list of the indefinite pronouns.

Anyone can swim.

No one sings like Bonnie Coke.

Indefinite Reference This error involves using certain pronouns to indicate nothing in particular. Sure, there are some instances where this use is acceptable as in "It is raining."

> *It* behooves you to behave. (Really?)

Indicative Mood A basic verb form that tells the reader that the verb indicates or points out something about the subject (or actor) of the sentence (see Appendix Four for a complete conjugation of the indicative mood). The verb in this mood is ACTIVE.

> Gail Snow (subject) directs (verb) several agencies at the Town Offices in Madison, Connecticut. (Notice how the verb "directs" *indicates* what the subject (Gail Snow) is performing.)
>
> Bob "Rocky" Johnson (subject) wiggles (verb) along the deck as he (subject) demonstrates (verb) the "Block Island Shuffle" to entice a striped bass toward a lure.

Indirect Object A word, phrase, or clause that receives action from the verb in an indirect manner. One might say that the indirect object is an OBJECT OF THE PREPOSITION—without the preposition. The word *to* or *for* seems to be missing.

> Throw the baby (indirect object) over the fence a glass (direct object) of water. (Obviously, the baby did not get thrown, but the glass of water did; therefore, the glass receives the action directly, the baby indirectly. Notice how "to" could be inserted between "throw" and "the baby."

Infinitive Phrase A group of words that begins with an infinitive and contains a modifier, and/or an object.

> Greg O'Connor wanted *to play in the Masters* but did not qualify.
>
> Jack O'Connor, *to demand the attention he deserves*, frequently shouts at bartenders to hurry up.

Interjection A part of speech that shows some type of emotion and really cannot be classified under any other part of speech. The Batman series and comic strip frequently used "Pow," "Ouch," and so on.

> "*My word!*" exclaimed Cindy Williams. "My husband actually came straight home from playing golf and cut the lawn!"

Interrogative Pronoun A pronoun usually used at the beginning of a question. *Who* or *whom* or *what* usually introduce a question.

> "What are you up to?" Cindy Williams asked her husband.
>
> Why are store clerks more than likely to respond with "No problem" instead of "You're welcome" when someone thanks them?

Linking Verbs These verbs link a *subject* with a *noun or adjective.* They are **appear, seem, feel, look, smell, taste, remain, go, stay, become, grow, turn, sound,** and **get.**

> Pete **appears** *wise* when looking for fishing holes.
>
> *Jeannie Chan* **became** a *princess* in the annual dramatic production.

Misplaced Modifier Any kind of adjective or adverb not in its correct place. A misplaced modifier either does not make sense or creates an impossible situation.

> Fred Nichols once bought a horse and a car **that won its first six races**. (Was it the car or the horse?)
>
> Sharlene Ordway **only** visits Madison when there is a reunion. ("Only" should be placed after "Madison.")

Modifier A word, phrase, or clause that alters, changes, limits, describes, or modifies a noun or pronoun. Thus, the word *crossword* is modified—that is, changed from an ordinary crossword—when *London Times* is attached to it.

Mood A grammatical term applied to verbs. The different moods are indicative active, indicative passive, progressive, emphatic, and subjunctive.

Noncountable Nouns Those nouns that cannot be defined with "a" or "an" and usually have no plural: *facetiousness, impetuousness, poverty, peace*.

Noun A word, phrase, or clause that functions as a subject, direct object, object of the preposition, indirect object, or predicate noun.

Noun Clause A clause that functions as a subject, direct object, indirect object, object of the preposition, or predicate noun.

Object of the Preposition A noun or pronoun that is joined by a preposition to some other word in the sentence.

> Julius Biehler <u>photographs</u> *in* his <u>spare time</u> the flora and fauna near his house.
>
> Dale Holdridge <u>drove</u> racing cars *at* <u>Lyme Rock</u>.

Paragraph A unit of words that make up a body of writing. Paragraphs can be long or short, usually follow some kind of plan, and have details arranged in a certain way. See Chapter Five for examples.

Parallel Structure All sorts of terms fit the definition: balance, same looking terms, same grammatical structures, and so on. Basically, parallel structure is using like grammatical terms to express ideas that are coupled or go beyond two.

> John and Peggy Doffek *live* in Somers, *winter* in Florida, and *travel* to foreign countries. (verbs in a series)

> Janet Schrensky not *only sings beautiful melodies* but *also paints gorgeous landscapes.* (verbs with correlative conjunctions)

Participial Phrase Every verb has four principal parts: the present (*bring*), the past (*brought*), the past participle (*brought*), and the present participle (*bringing*). Every dictionary gives the principal parts for every verb. When the past participle and the present participle are used without helping verbs, these parts of verbs become verbals—either adjectives (past and present participle) or nouns (present participle only).

> *Wearing* (present participle—adjective) a beautiful Dior creation, Cathy Devaux attended the Hand '55 Reunion in a limo.

> Ron Hick loves *sailing* (present participle—noun) on Long Island Sound.

> *Torn* (past participle—adjective) between playing golf and attending the reunion, Bob Kelley agonized about his decision.

Passive Voice The subject of the sentence is acted upon—therefore passive.

> Frank Rettich *was selected* by the Town Committee to investigate vernal pools.
>
> Devereaux Knox *was honored* by the Navy Seals.

Past Perfect Tense A tense that indicates past action *before* some other time in the past. In other words, two past actions in one sentence—one happening before the other. (See Appendix Four for the conjugation of verb forms.)

> Don Williams *had sailed* (past action happening first) to Booth Bay Harbor before he *docked* (past action second) in Stonington.

Past Tense One of the six tenses of any verb. This tense indicates completed action that is done with.

> Pat Williams *fertilized* (over and done with—not for nothing) her garden once in the spring.

Personal Pronoun A pronoun that takes the place of a person. Although *it* is considered a personal pronoun, this one really cannot take the place of a person.

> Cynthia Hallman visits the school named after *her* father, Robert H. Brown.

Phrase A group of words that does not have a subject and verb. The types of phrases are prepositional, participial, gerund, infinitive, and appositive.

Predicate Noun A noun that renames the subject.

> <u>Rusty Nyborg</u> was the *president* of the San Francisco Bay Pilot's Association.

Present Tense

Present Perfect Tense This tense indicates a time in the past that extends to the present.

> Joe Andrukaitis *has traveled* extensively throughout America. (See how this verb implies that the action not only extends to the present but also hints that the travel will continue.)

Preposition A word that joins a noun or pronoun to some other word in the sentence. There is a list of all the prepositions you'll ever need in Appendix Five.

Progressive Mood Another ACTIVE verb form that does something besides showing action. This mood causes the verb to imply ongoing action.

> Connie Donkin (subject) was visiting (verb) her friends in Falmouth, Massachusetts. (Notice that the subject "was visiting," indicates that the action of "visiting" is ongoing.)

Pronoun A word that takes the place of a noun There are several categories: personal subjective, personal objective, personal possessive, indefinite, demonstrative, relative, reflexive (and intensive). (See the lists in Appendix One.)

Proper Noun A noun that designates a specific and therefore demands capitalization: *New York Mets*, *David Wright*, *Jose Reyes*, *Grammar the Easy Way*, *Durham High School*.

Relative Pronoun A pronoun that relates to another word—but not to a general idea.

> Jack Law, *who* rides canoes up and down the Housatonic River, also rides dirt bikes in competition.

But the following is incorrectly used:

> Ann Barber Nyborg runs the Whaler Vineyard, volunteers for Meals on Wheels, and enters quilting contests weekly. *This* keeps her busy.

Verbal A word that looks like a verb but functions as another part of speech.

> *Possessing* (adjective) qualities that are envied by her friends, Sue Quatrano humbly accepts all accolades, especially concerning her fishing.
>
> *Fishing* (noun) in the Everglades demanded more than Frank Quatrano realized.
>
> *To win* (adjective) friends and influence people, Bobby Bushnell donates fliptops to needy children.

Appendix Eight

COMPARATIVE AND SUPERLATIVE

Adjectives have three forms: The first is the form that simply modifies or changes a noun into something more specific. Thus *staff* becomes something definite when *teaching* is added to it. Add another form of an adjective and the word *staff* becomes even more specific: *the teaching staff of Durham High School.* If we insert a date, then the *1965 teaching staff of Durham High School* leaves no doubts.

The **comparative** form adds *-er* to one-syllable words when two items are being compared: *sicker*, as in "Of his sister and him, he was the **sicker**." If the adjective has more than one syllable, usually *more* is used to show the comparison: "Growing up, he was **more sickly** than his sister."

When there are more than two items involved, the **superlative** form is used. In one-syllable words, adding *-est* is correct. Words with more than one syllable usually demand the use of *most*. For example, *fastest, hardest,* or *coolest; most pretentious, most beautiful,* or *most ulcerogenic.*"

Sports sometimes defies logic with the accepted *winningest* as in "Grover Cleveland Alexander, in 1915 and 1916, was the **winningest** pitcher in the Major Leagues with a total of 64 wins."

Appendix Nine

READING PROGRAM TO INCREASE READING AND WRITING VOCABULARY

Do not read over anything you do not know

This technique or reading plan will increase one's vocabulary, make one a better reader, and enable one to write better.

"Word attack," basic vocabulary for any reading teacher, has been around a long time. However, it works both ways: Readers can "attack" a word or the word can "attack" readers and cause ignorance of an author's message because the meaning of the sentence and most likely the paragraph will not make sense.

In other words, stop, look (up), and listen while the voice of the dictionary takes over the pronunciation and the meaning of unfamiliar words. Incidentally, *Webster's Collegiate Dictionary*, eleventh edition, now comes with a CD that does pronounce the words looked up.

Read the following excerpt from "Bartleby the Scrivener" by Herman Melville:

> One winter day, I presented Turkey with a highly
> respectable-looking coat of my own—a padded gray coat
> of most comfortable warmth, and which buttoned straight
> up from the knee to the neck. I thought Turkey would appre-
> ciate the favor, and <u>abate</u> his <u>rashness</u> and <u>obstreperousness</u>
> of afternoons. But no; I <u>verily</u> believe that buttoning

himself up in so <u>downy</u> and blanket-like a coat had a
<u>pernicious</u> effect upon him—upon the same principle that
too much oats are bad for horses. In fact, precisely as a <u>rash</u>,
<u>restive</u> horse is said to feel his oats, so Turkey felt his coat.
It made him <u>insolent</u>. He was a man <u>prosperity</u> harmed.

How many of the boldfaced words did you not know? If your
answer is "None!" then perhaps this program is not for you. If you
said **obstreperousness** and **restive,** did you look them up in a reli-
able dictionary? If the answer is No! then you have **"read over
something you do not know."**

Whatever and whenever you read, there will be times when a
word that you do not know appears, but rather than slow yourself
down, you continue reading and guess at the meaning, only to find
later your guess was incorrect. Make your mind up, then, to look
up unfamiliar words as they occur.

Here's the program:

- Purchase a hard cover notebook, one that will take a beating
  because you will use it every day.

- Set aside an hour a day to read whatever you want—even your English assignment or biology or earth science or *Seventeen* or whatever strikes your fancy—but read for one hour.

- When you see a word you do not know, look it up, make the definition fit the context (the author intends the meaning of the word *only* one way), and then write the word and the definition and some of the context into the notebook—and continue reading—but "**Do not read over anything you do not know.**"

> **Example: pernicious**—highly injurious or destructive: DEADLY. Syn: baneful, noxious, deleterious, detrimental. . . . coat had a **pernicious** effect . . .

Purchase a Reliable Dictionary

Poorly written, cheap dictionaries are a waste of money, but they can quickly start a fire. Choose one that will provide a lifetime of service like

Merriam Webster's Collegiate Dictionary, Eleventh Edition, with the CD that pronounces the words

Random House Collegiate Dictionary

American Heritage Dictionary

Oxford English Dictionary, now on a CD

All of these dictionaries are respected in the reading, writing, scholarly community. These resources also contain "Manuals of Style" and "Grammatical References." And the more you use the dictionary of your choice, the more proficient in language you will become.

Appendix Ten

ANSWERS TO WHO, WHOM QUIZ

1. Whom (Mary Jane Fegen is the subject; *whom* is the direct object.)
2. Who (Subject of "did")
3. Who (predicate pronoun renaming it—referring to student)
4. Whoever (subject of the noun clause)
5. Whomever (direct object of "thought")
6. Whoever (subject of the clause)
7. Who (predicate pronoun renaming "catcher")
8. Whom (object of "will")
9. Whoever (subject of "would listen")
10. Whom (object of "do trust")

INDEX